The Open University

Block 5
Creating Nations

Clive Emsley, Paul Lawrence and Michael Drake

This publication forms part of an Open University course *A200 Exploring History: Medieval to Modern 1400–1900.*. Details of this and other Open University courses can be obtained from the Student Registration and Enquiry Service, The Open University, PO Box 197, Milton Keynes, MK7 6BJ, United Kingdom: tel. +44 (0)870 333 4340, email general-enquiries@open.ac.uk

Alternatively, you may visit the Open University website at http://www.open.ac.uk where you can learn more about the wide range of courses and packs offered at all levels by The Open University.

To purchase a selection of Open University course materials visit http://www.ouw.co.uk, or contact Open University Worldwide, Michael Young Building, Walton Hall, Milton Keynes MK7 6AA, United Kingdom for a brochure. tel. +44 (0)1908 858785; fax +44 (0)1908 858787; email ouwenq@open.ac.uk

The Open University
Walton Hall, Milton Keynes
MK7 6AA

First published 2007

Edited and designed by The Open University.

Typeset by The Open University

Printed and bound in the United Kingdom by Bell & Bain Ltd., Glasgow

ISBN 978 0 7492 16863

1.1

B/a200_Block5_el1l_N9780749216863

Mixed Sources
Product group from well-managed forests and other controlled sources
www.fsc.org Cert no. TT-COC-002769
© 1996 Forest Stewardship Council

The paper used in this publication contains pulp sourced from forests independently certified to the Forest Stewardship Council (FSC) principles and criteria. Chain of custody certification allows the pulp from these forests to be tracked to the end use (see www.fsc-uk.org).

CONTENTS

INTRODUCTION

Clive Emsley

WHAT YOU NEED TO STUDY THIS BLOCK

- Units 17–20
- *Course Guide*
- *Visual Sources*
- Anthology documents
- Secondary sources on the A200 website
- TMA 05

Learning outcomes

When you have finished this block you will have:

- gained some significant historical information about economic, political and social change in Europe from the late eighteenth century to roughly 1870

- extended your knowledge of the three themes of the course, specifically in a new time period

- acquired additional information to enable you to distinguish how and why the subject matter of these themes can differ across time

- developed your skills in working with and analysing different types of historical source material.

INTRODUCTION TO THE THEMES OF THE BLOCK

This block covers the period from the end of the eighteenth century to the last third of the nineteenth. This was a period that witnessed if not the end, then certainly the beginning of the end of the old regime (or, in the commonly used French term, *ancien régime*) in Europe. It also saw the beginning of what we now understand to be the modern nation state.

The old regime (and perhaps 'old regimes' would be better) contained the vestiges of feudalism. You have already encountered the concept of 'feudalism' in the discussion of the fourteenth century in Block 1. The concept survived in varying forms, usually quite different from its medieval shape, and with varying degrees of economic and social importance into the eighteenth century and, according to some historians, beyond. The old regime was characterised by a rural economy dominated by a hereditary, privileged nobility. The fortunes of the nobility were based on land. The nobles were closely tied to the leaders of the church and, under the monarch, they dominated economically, politically and socially. The new regime, which emerged at a very different rate in different countries and regions, was increasingly characterised by industrial economies involving the mass production of many goods in factories. It saw a significant rise of merchant princes, whose wealth was based on the new industries or on new financial structures and systems rather than on land. Traditional privilege came under attack. The new regime was also characterised by states that began to treat all men as equal under their laws (though gender distinctions remained sharp and were sometimes intensified by new laws). 'Citizens' replaced 'subjects' and increasingly these citizens began to play an acknowledged part in political debate. Citizens were encouraged to see themselves as members of a nation state. But some radical critics of the newly emerging regime and of the new economic and social system encouraged them to see themselves as members of a social class. ? ?

It is illustrative of the changes that occurred in the half century following the storming of the Bastille (14 July 1789) and the French revolutionaries' abolition of 'feudalism' and noble privilege (4 August 1789) that, during this period, the English language (along with most European languages) either acquired the following words or else acquired the modern meanings of these words: 'capitalism', 'conservative', 'factory', 'industrialist', 'industry', 'liberal', middle class', 'nationality', 'police', 'proletariat', 'railway', 'revolution', 'socialism', 'statistics', 'strike', 'working class'. In the early 1960s, the historian E. J. Hobsbawm characterised this period as that of the '"dual revolution" – the French Revolution of 1789 and the contemporaneous (British) Industrial Revolution' (Hobsbawm, 1962). A cluster of historians and social scientists have also seen in the French Revolution the beginnings of what some have thought of as 'the age of nationalism', when individuals, now citizens of a state rather than subjects of a monarch, began to identify themselves first and foremost with their 'nation'. The concepts of the dual revolution and the emergence of nationalism and the nation state implicitly underlie much of what follows. But to the fore are the principal themes of the course, treated, as usual, with varying emphases in the different units.

The block begins with a discussion of the impact of the French Revolution and the subsequent domination of Europe by Napoleon. We are not going to give you a detailed account of either – there is neither the time nor the space, and such detail can be followed up by reading a short, up-to-date textbook (e.g. Jones, 2003). The principal focus of the first unit (Unit 17) is state formation. It addresses how new ideas about the state were developed and put into practice in a variety of different contexts. These new ideas, together with a new kind of war involving mass armies and appeals to 'the nation', also raise issues about shifting beliefs and ideologies during the period. From developments in the state, its politics and its involvement in war, we move on to the growth of industrial societies (Unit 18). The discussion here turns much more towards producers and consumers, but it also explores how beliefs and ideologies were moulded by economic change and by people's understanding of that change. States and nations sought new forms of legitimacy as a result of the changes discussed in Units 17 and 18. Closely related to these changes, from the mid nineteenth century a clutch of artists, poets and men from the new academic subject of history sought to establish and portray the origins, and the unique qualities, of individual nations. This is the focus of the third unit (Unit 19); its key emphasis is on beliefs and ideologies, but obviously it links with state formation. The final unit in the block (Unit 20) provides a case study of how one particular form of knowledge – the new discipline of history – inter-related with ideas of nationalism across the nineteenth century. It is worth stressing here that in Unit 20 you will find the evidence presented to you is the work of historians but, rather than reading this work as secondary source material for a narrative of events and interpretation, you will be reading it as a primary source. Here you will see that it is not so much the events of the narrative that are important, but the respective authors' hidden (as well as quite explicit) attitudes and assumptions about 'nations' and 'nationalism'.

For a variety of reasons the new, bureaucratic nation states were keen to collect information on their economies and their populations. The block concludes with a short essay on a key aspect of this kind of information – national censuses – exploring how and why such censuses were created and contrasting the kinds of information sought. Your work in this section is also designed to develop your use of IT in historical study.

REFERENCES

Hobsbawm, E.J. (1962) *The Age of Revolution: Europe from 1789 to 1848*, London, Weidenfeld & Nicolson.

Jones, P.M. (2003) *The French Revolution 1787–1804*, London, Longman.

Clive Emsley

A NEW STATE: A NEW PEOPLE

EXERCISE

I want you to start this unit with a careful reading of two documents: Anthology Document 5.1, 'Decree of the National Convention (*levée en masse*), 23 August 1793' and Anthology Document 5.2, '*Le chant du départ* (The song of departure), *c.*1794', by Marie-Joseph de Chénier. I recognise that I am asking you to read these without you necessarily having any idea of the context in which they were written. I will try to fill in the context as best I can in the space available in what follows, but read the two documents carefully now and note down answers to the following questions.

1   What kind of war do the French think they are fighting?

2   Who or what do they think they are fighting for?

3   Who is identified as being involved on the opposite sides of the conflict?

4   (A difficult and very general question.) Would you say that these documents suggest a different kind of war from the kinds that you have looked at earlier in the course?

Spend about 15 minutes on this exercise.

SPECIMEN ANSWER

1   The documents imply that this is some kind of total war in which every individual, young and old, male and female, is involved and has a part to play.

2   The song, in particular, stresses the idea of a war for the republic, for peace and for liberty.

3   A sovereign people (the French) are ranged against enemies variously described as kings, tyrants, feudalism and oppression. The French see themselves as offering an example to the world.

4   Earlier in the course we have come across wars involving monarchs and peoples and religious beliefs, but we have not seen anything quite as explicit as these calls for an entire people to participate. Also, here a 'sovereign' people is involved. The French are fighting for *their* republic, not a king; and as a *sovereign* people, the ultimate authority in this republic is with the people.

A nation state embarked on a war with its citizens motivated by ideas of a sovereign people? Well, perhaps, and that is one of the key issues that we are going to explore in this unit.

When you have successfully completed this unit you should have acquired knowledge sufficient to enable you to engage with questions concerning:

• the impact of war and revolution on state formation in the late eighteenth and early nineteenth centuries

- the inter-relationship between war and revolution and shifting beliefs and ideologies during the period.

You will also have developed further your abilities to:

- analyse historical documents
- think critically about historical issues.

The popular image of the French Revolution begins with the violent storming of the Bastille on 14 July 1789 and moves very rapidly from there to the overthrow of the monarchy and the mass guillotining of aristocrats. Violent events are more exciting than political debates and theorising. In 1789, a bankrupt monarchy was forced to call an assembly that had not met for over 150 years in an attempt to balance the books. A majority in the assembly was not prepared to bail out the regime without some concessions. The monarchy was forced to go along with the assembly's demands and, fired with Enlightenment rationalism, the early revolutionaries embarked on a massive programme of reform. The monarchy was to be constitutional rather than absolutist. The entire administrative structure of the state was to be reorganised on rational grounds. Men were to hold posts because of ability rather than birth. A new legal structure was prepared in which all were supposed to be equal before the law and, whatever their social standing, were to be subject to the same sorts of punishment. Old administrative boundaries that appeared to have no rational foundation were replaced by *départements* of roughly similar size, each carefully subdivided. New local administrations were to be decentralised. The church was to be nationalised and the clergy, rather than owing a potential allegiance to a non-French ruler – the pope – who lived outside France, were to be made salaried servants of the state.

Reforms of such magnitude did not go unchallenged. Among the principal opponents was the monarchy that did not take kindly to the loss of absolutist powers. Louis XVI was married to the sister of the Holy Roman Emperor. The emperor, and other major European monarchs, looked on at events in France with some concern. One of their peers had been significantly deprived of authority; France was a major power and its monarchy had been a model for other princes to follow. There were concerns that similar events might occur elsewhere. But there were also hopes that, if France fell apart internally or was defeated in war, then there might be pickings. The European monarchs began to make threatening noises about events in France. The French assembly responded in the spring of 1792 by declaring war, first on the emperor and then on most of the other monarchs of Europe. Significantly, the French assembly declared war on monarchs, not on peoples. French revolutionary activists had begun to think that their revolution was a model for others to follow.

Initially the war went badly for the French. Under the old regime, army officers were noblemen and many of these left the country as *émigrés* once the fighting started – some even went before. Inside France there were concerns about 'aristocrats' (and the term was often used to cover non-nobles with counter-revolutionary ideas) seeking to undermine the country from within. These concerns led to the overthrow of the monarchy by popular insurrection in August 1792. Prominent in this insurrection were volunteer units that had come from different parts of France to defend Paris against invading armies; and notable among these units was a battalion from the southern port city of Marseilles who had adopted a war song as ferocious as that of Chénier.

The tide of war turned in favour of the French towards the end of 1792, and their deputies in what was now the National Convention began issuing defiant challenges to European monarchs and promising assistance to any people struggling to be free. But the pressure of war demanded men with which to fight it. On 24 February, the Convention announced a levy of 300,000 men for the armies. Then, on 23 August, came the decree of the *levée en masse*.

EXERCISE

Look at the following extracts from two folksongs:

> Na neus mui a zermoniou, vijil na Kovesion
> Ol é mant bet distrujet dré eurz an Nasion
> Ne glever nemet touet pep sort Komozou lubik
> Setu eno ar beden a ra ar Republik.

(There are no sermons, vigils or confessions. / They have all been destroyed by the order of the nation. / The only oaths to be heard are all kinds of lewd words / that are the prayers of the republic.)

> Chervijein en Nasion zou dra disoursi
> Kalon er Vretoned zou lan a velkoni ...

> Adieu de vanniélieu, de groézieu hon ilis,
> Rak berpet é vou ret gobér en ecsersis.

(Serving the nation is a disagreeable thing, / the hearts of Bretons are full of sorrow ... / Farewell to the banners and the cross of our church, / now we must spend all our time at drill.)

(Quoted in Emsley, 1988, p. 51)

1 What language is this written in? (It is probably not a language with which you are familiar, but there is a clue in the second extract.)

2 How do the sentiments expressed here compare with those in the two documents that you read at the beginning of this section?

Spend about 5 minutes on this exercise.

SPECIMEN ANSWER

1 It is Breton.

2 The sentiments are not as enthusiastic towards the nation and republic as those encountered in the earlier song or in the stirring words of the *levée en masse*.

Resistance to the levies of 1793 was particularly hostile in the west of France – in Brittany, and in the region immediately south, the Vendée. The resistance here built on peasant hostility to the townsfolk in the region and to the Revolution's religious policies, sparking a full-scale rebellion that was fought with appalling brutality on both sides and was harshly crushed. This was, perhaps, the most marked instance of the revolutionary regime in Paris forcing its policies on recalcitrant groups and regions, but it was not unique. The Revolution had begun as an attempt to rationalise and decentralise government. Under pressure of war, however, the old regime aspiration of focusing power at the centre was re-established and vigorously enforced. Under the rule of a successful military man, Napoleon Bonaparte, the centralisation policy was developed still further. Yet, while the centralisation was re-established, many of the liberal reforming ideas of the early stages of the Revolution remained. Government posts were no longer venal. While mayors, local police chiefs, magistrates, departmental administrators and so forth ceased to be elected by the local community and were appointed by central government, there continued to be some genuflection towards the idea of the sovereign people. The new constitution resulting from *coup d'état* that brought Citizen-General Bonaparte to power was submitted to a plebiscite in January 1800. Plebiscites were also held to approve Bonaparte becoming consul for life (1802) and emperor (1804), and then to approve the new constitution, the *Acte additionnel*, that he brought in during his brief return to power in 1815. The votes may have been rigged, but it was quite new for a head of state to present himself and new governing structures for popular approval. Moreover, even when the revolutionary and later Napoleonic armies were embarked on wars of conquest rather than the self-preservation of 1792–94, the publicists and many within the army, and the administrators and bureaucrats who followed in its wake, continued to think of themselves as part of *la grande nation* who were bringing enlightenment and liberty to less-fortunate peoples.

Napoleon Bonaparte (1769–1821) was born into the minor Corsican nobility. He went to military school in France and was gazetted as artillery officer in 1785. The French revolutionary wars enabled him to rise rapidly in rank. A general in 1796, he commanded French forces in Italy with dazzling success. He led an expedition to Egypt in 1798. Returning in 1799, he engaged in a successful coup that resulted in his appointment as first consul. In 1802, he became consul for life and in 1804, emperor; each elevation was confirmed by plebiscite. A series of successful campaigns brought much of Europe into his empire: either formally incorporated or as allies and satellites. A disastrous invasion of Russia in 1812 brought a backlash forcing his abdication in 1814. He was established as emperor of Elba, but returned to France in 1815. Defeated at Waterloo, at the end of what is commonly described as 'the Hundred Days', he was compelled to abdicate a second time and on this occasion was exiled to the island of St Helena, where he died under British guard.

THE SUCCESS OF THE NEW STATE

General Bonaparte took power in November 1799, after a decade of war, civil war (in the Vendée for example) and revolution. What do you suppose he needed to do to secure his position?

Spend about 5 minutes on this exercise.

One obvious thing that he needed to do was to get rid of potential threats to his position. In addition, considering the upheaval of revolution, civil war and war, it can be argued that what many people in France wanted in 1799 was internal security and peace. So he also needed to achieve these.

The Napoleonic state in France

There are two things that stand out in the popular conception of the Napoleonic state and that need some qualification – first, what appears to be its bellicose nature and, second, its internal security system.

Napoleon was an extremely able military commander. As a result of the military successes of the revolutionary and then his own armies, the internal boundaries of Europe were redrawn. But Napoleon was not always at war. Indeed, within little more than a year of taking power he had brought peace to continental Europe and was encouraging more *émigrés* from the Revolution to return home and participate in rebuilding the country as soldiers and members of central and local administrations. Just over two years after his coup, he had come to an agreement with the pope which, while it maintained the dominance of the French state over the Catholic Church in the country, brought to an end the mutual hostility between church and state that had characterised most of the revolutionary period. Napoleon's armies were engaged in no major fighting in Europe between the summer of 1800 and that of 1805. Conscription and new taxes to fight wars were not to weigh seriously on the French people until the end of the decade.

The Napoleonic state has been described as a police state. In some measure it was, though not in the sense of twentieth-century police states, and one historian has suggested that, to avoid the modern connotations, a better term to describe the internal Napoleonic system is 'security state' (Brown, 1997). A minister of police presided over the network of *commissaires* established in all the major towns of the empire who were required to send regular reports on public opinion as well as crime and public order. In Paris, under the newly established prefect of police, forty-eight *commissaires* performed similar functions. The 'security state' could behave with brutality and complete disregard for due process. The kidnapping and execution of the duc d'Enghien in 1804 was the most extreme instance of this. There was political surveillance and some people were held under preventive detention. But preventive detention also had a significant non-political use: families concerned about the behaviour of a disruptive or libertine son, daughter or other relation could request the prefect have the offender held in prison without charge for a fixed period. The military police that patrolled the roads and small towns of provincial France, the *gendarmerie*, was reformed and revivified in the months following Napoleon's coup. Backed by the army, it was deployed against the brigands that infested many regions of France – and bear in mind that 'brigand' is one of those words that can embrace a variety of offenders. In France in the late 1790s, brigands could be a gang of smugglers or highway robbers, a gang of political terrorists seeking revenge for some action taken during the revolutionary upheavals or seeking to reverse the most recent *coup d'état*. They could also be armed army deserters, or Vendéan or Breton counter-revolutionaries, or any combination of such individuals. The *gendarmes* helped to bring, and then to maintain, order in the countryside. They became part of a new unspoken but reciprocal agreement between state and people. The *gendarmes* brought order. They also assisted people in the event of a flood or fire, or the threat of wild animals – bears and wolves were still to be found in parts of France. But the state also used its *gendarmes* to enforce the reciprocal side of the coin. *Gendarmes* might enforce the state's promise of protection and security to its citizens, but they also brought in the conscripts and protected the state's tax collectors.

Taxes under the old regime had been collected by a private corporation of wealthy financiers who made agreements with the king to produce a fixed amount of money for him over a set period. The 'tax farmers', as they were called, were allowed to keep any money that that they collected over and above the amount promised in the agreement. Under the new regime, tax collection became the task of people employed directly by the state; the senior receivers were required to post security bonds and were subject to inspection by treasury officials. Taxation was principally direct and levied on land and personal property; under the new regime there were attempts to ensure that it was fair and equitable. It was only towards the end of the first decade of the nineteenth century that serious deficits began to appear, principally as a result of Napoleon's military adventures. His government's response was a series of indirect taxes on commodities such as alcohol, playing cards, salt and tobacco.

But the new state did not run simply on reasonably effective policing and tax collection. An efficient bureaucracy that was trained for the job administered the new administrative structure of the state. There was still nepotism and favouritism but, from 1803, young men from good families and with potential were brought into central government as *auditeurs* of the Council of State. Here they provided assistance to the council and to the ministries. The post of *auditeur* itself was the first step on the ladder to the top administrative posts, such as the prefect of a *département*. The prefects were the instruments of the emperor, supervising every aspect of the region under their control, preparing lists of recommendations for mayors and *commissaires* from which central government could make appointments and sending in regular reports of the economic and political situation.

The early revolutionaries had set out to establish a criminal code under which all people were equal. They abolished the vestiges of feudalism that required peasants to labour for their lord and use his mill, his olive or wine press, and that gave some nobles the right to administer justice. The property of *émigrés* and of the church was seized by the state and sold off to those who could afford it; the purchasers included many peasants. The Napoleonic regime preserved these changes, cementing them most notably with a massive codification project that drew up a legal structure for all aspects of life. The Code Napoleon eventually combined a Civil Code (1804 and 1807), which was particularly important in preserving the Revolution's division of property and maintaining by law a patriarchal family structure, a Code of Civil Procedure (1806), a Commercial Code (1807), a Code of Criminal Procedure (1808) and a Criminal Code (1810).

EXERCISE

Anthology Document 5.3, 'The Napoleonic Code, 21 March 1804', comprises a number of extracts from the Civil Code. Read it now and answer the following questions.

1   I have just noted the revolutionaries creating a criminal code that established equality before the law. But how far is equality established by this code?

2   Is there a group within society that is singled out here for having authority over others?

3   What does the code have to say with regard to property?

Spend about 20 minutes on this exercise.

SPECIMEN ANSWER

1   All Frenchmen have civil rights and this is extended to those born of foreign parents in France, once they have achieved their majority. However, and this is discussed more fully with reference to the next question, some individuals are more equal than others, particularly the male heads of families.

2   By the various clauses included among the extracts in Anthology Document 5.3, it is clear that the male heads of families were given significant authority over their children, their wives and the property of their wives. The code also formally sanctioned a double standard for infidelity.

3   The code established the absolute right of ownership for individuals holding property. The code states that, upon death, an individual's heirs are to inherit equal portions (clause 745). [I don't expect you to have known this, or to have deduced it from the documents, but partible inheritance had existed in some regions of France in the Middle Ages. The code ensured that it remained in existence (though it was often got round) as France developed a modern, industrialised economy.]

Some of these issues will recur in this block. It is important to note here, for example, that any individual born in France was given the right to be a French citizen – something which runs counter to any ideas of nationalism based on ethnicity. There had not been gender equality under the old regime, but the Civil Code established in law the superiority of the patriarch, the family's male head, and put women, especially wives, in a subservient role. Wives could hold no private property; and they could use infidelity as grounds for divorce only if a husband brought his mistress to live in the family home – in contrast to the husband's ability to divorce his wife on the grounds of her infidelity. In many respects, this was a step back from some of the progressive legislation of the early stages of the Revolution; in 1816, the restored Bourbons were to put the clock back even further by abolishing divorce and thereby re-establishing the situation that had existed before 1789. Establishing an individual's rights to the absolute ownership of their property cemented the Revolution's abolition of feudalism and any duties of feudal obligation and servitude dependent on the possession of a particular piece of land. This also helped to guarantee the ownership of those who had acquired either land of nobles who had fled the Revolution or church land. The Bourbons did not seek to change this situation, recognising the potential for trouble that such an action might provoke.

The Napoleonic state developed other ideas espoused by the revolutionaries, though not always successfully or in the way that was originally hoped. The men of 1789 believed that the state should take responsibility for education. They wanted a secularised, national system. Through its policy of nationalising the church, the Revolution brought about the collapse of the education provided by the church. The chaos of revolution and the cost and upheaval of war meant that little positive was done to amend the situation before Napoleon's seizure of power. The educational policies established during the empire were directed towards creating civil and military leaders. Primary education was neglected, as was the education of girls. The lasting achievement was the creation of *lycées* in which government-appointed teachers taught a uniform curriculum to middle-class boys.

The revolutionaries had also aspired to stamp out poverty, indigence and begging. Welfare was not to be freely provided to the able bodied, however; it was to be given only in return for work. Again the treatment of the church disrupted the old system of poor relief and again internal disorder and the cost of war impeded the welfare development proposed by the revolutionaries. Moreover, the state's decision to provide for wounded and disabled soldiers, of whom the wars ensured there was a large number, skewed the system. Here the Napoleonic regime made little change and welfare provision remained in a sorry state. The restoration of the Bourbon monarchy in 1815 brought the church back more fully into poor relief, and private donation and charity continued to dominate rather than the state.

The Napoleonic state beyond France

As a result of Napoleon's domination of Europe, many of the changes described above spread, in varying degrees, far beyond the frontiers of France. You should read the following paragraph with three maps from the *Visual Sources*, Plates 17.1–17.3, in front of you to get a feel for the enormous changes wrought in Europe by the revolutionary and Napoleonic wars. If you are not familiar with the whereabouts of Bavaria, Baden, Piedmont, the Papal

States, and so on, you should keep the maps close by you for the rest of the unit.

Plates 17.1 and 17.2 illustrate the boundary changes brought about by war from the beginning of the Revolution to the peak of Napoleon's domination of Europe in 1810. The empire itself comprised 130 *départements* including modern Belgium (annexed 1793–95), parts of the Rhineland (1797), parts of Italy (1802, 1807 and 1809), parts of Switzerland (1798 and 1810) and the Netherlands (1810). In addition, there were satellite states and dependants. Some of these, like Spain and the kingdom of Italy, were ruled by Napoleon's relatives. Others, such as the three major states of the Confederation of the Rhine (Baden, Bavaria and Württemberg), owed their geographic size and structure to his boundary making. The Congress of Vienna redrew some of the boundaries in the wake of Napoleon's final defeat in 1815. But, as you can see from Plate 17.3, the congress did not turn the clock back to 1789. The old French frontiers were largely restored, but the reorganisation of Germany maintained the major states that Napoleon had constructed in 1803. What the maps cannot show is how much also remained of the internal organisation of the states that had been part of the French empire or its satellites and allies.

Wherever the French settled for any period of time, the vestiges of feudalism were abolished, though this did not necessarily benefit the peasantry. It was the same with policies towards the church. Clerical lands were sold off, but often it was not the peasantry who could afford to buy and many were pushed into the position of landless labourers. The promise of security from brigands and assistance in time of natural threat or disaster were benefits that most could welcome; but conscription of young men for the army and the efficient collection of taxes were not necessarily regarded as an acceptable price of such security At the same time, the French had established a legal system by which all, from noble to peasant, from cleric to shopkeeper, were fundamentally equal before the law. Wherever the system had been imposed, it largely survived Napoleon's defeat.

Some of the territories that had been incorporated into France for almost twenty years were keen to maintain French structures in preference to those of their new masters. Well-to-do Rhinelanders, for example, who had done relatively well under Napoleon through educational opportunities, the suppression of banditry and the chance to purchase church lands, strongly and successfully resisted Prussian attempts to replace French law with that of Prussia. In a similar way, when Belgium secured its independence from the Netherlands in 1830, it largely restored French legal practices and adopted a singularly liberal constitution.

States that had been reconstituted by the French had also taken the opportunity to reform themselves internally, incorporating and reshaping to their own needs some of what they saw as the best French practices. The rulers of Baden, Bavaria and Württemberg were all notable in this respect. They sought to remove any group or institution that competed with them for a monopoly of power. The church was an obvious competitor and found much of its property

Handwritten marginal notes:

A NATION STATE?

Was it the "institutions of state" that make the state.

EXECUTIVE
LEGISLATURE
JUDICIARY

"all equal before the law"?

TAX system?
EDUCATION
police system.

cultural issues that led to 'nationalism'

sequestrated and sold off. Independent cities were particularly vulnerable to these monarchs and those that survived the centralising policies of the French themselves fell prey to monopolising monarchs. The imperial city of Augsburg, for example, kept its independence under the Napoleonic reorganisation of western Germany in 1803 but was occupied by Bavarian troops and incorporated into the Bavarian kingdom two years later. The monarchs were less successful in their moves against the nobility and gentry who, in many places, continued to maintain some of their seigniorial rights and the ability to appoint local judges and teachers. Nevertheless, the independent political power and authority of the nobility and gentry was increasingly identified as subordinate.

The French Revolution and Napoleon significantly changed the internal shape of Italy, but here, after 1815, there were no middle ranking states that survived like those in western and south-western Germany. Italy, moreover, was home to some monarchs who, on Napoleon's fall, were particularly eager to put back the clock. Victor Emmanuel, for example, who got back the Piedmontese region of his kingdom, professed the aim of abolishing all the French changes. Yet he found it in the interests of his kingdom and of his own authority to maintain the French-created tax inspectorate and to revive the French-created *gendarmerie*, albeit under the new name of the *carabinieri reali*. In the Papal States, the *Zelanti* were keen to go back to the privileges and practices of the past, even to the extent of abolishing the new fire brigade and street illumination. But the pope's secretary of state, Cardinal Ercole Consalvi, who preserved those French reforms that served to accentuate the glory of the pope and maintain his unquestioned supremacy as a secular ruler, moderated such reactionary extremism. Indeed, Consalvi also resisted attempts to restore the church lands that the French had confiscated and sold off to groups of investors. He reasoned that this had happened years before and that the reappropriation of those lands would only serve to create opposition and trouble.

Inspired by ideas of the Enlightenment, the initial French revolutionaries had wanted to abolish privilege and birth as the only route to power within the bureaucracy and to improve the way in which the French monarchy functioned. War had redirected their plans for a decentralised liberal system into a centralised and authoritarian one; but as the armies of the reorganised state proved, the new administrative structures were efficient and effective. The military destruction of the old order in Germany and Italy that followed enabled men with the same kind of Enlightenment ideas to achieve power under French patronage. Such winners, like Charles Frederick of Baden and Maximilian I Joseph of Bavaria, were not politically liberal but they were keen to enhance the power and efficiency of their territories. They surrounded themselves with able, similarly minded, ministers who seized the opportunities provided by the wars to reorganise and strengthen their positions with a raft of reforms cherry-picked from the French examples. Most of them conveniently changed sides as the fortunes of Napoleon waned, and when the French genie was finally put back in its bottle they continued in power and maintained their reorganisations. Others, like Consalvi, used the situation in 1815 as an opportunity to secure some of the changes dreamt of by reformers in their lands towards the end of the eighteenth century.

THE ALTERNATIVE STATE

Two states stand out as the most consistent enemies of revolutionary and Napoleonic France – Austria and Britain. The former was a land power, the latter a sea power. Austria sprawled across central Europe and, while several of its rulers during the eighteenth century had subscribed to the rational and progressive ideas of the Enlightenment, the emperor and his ministers had few constitutional constraints on their power. Britain, in contrast, had been a model for a number of Enlightenment thinkers. It was seen as a society that prided itself on its ideas of liberty, wherein there appeared to be a separation of powers between the executive, the legislature and the judiciary, and wherein the monarch's power was limited by lords and gentry in parliament. That said, however, and given what follows about the state structures, the wars were not fought simply over conceptions of the best form of government – there were also rivalries, hostilities and fears over economic and territorial matters. Debates about who or what were the principal causes of these wars could make a university course in themselves (and often do).

The reactionary state

Once again, turn to the maps in the *Visual Sources*, Plates 17.1–17.3. As you can see, from Plate 17.1, in 1789 the government in Vienna administered a range of territories across Europe: from the Austrian Netherlands (Belgium) in the west to Hungary in the east, from parts of Poland in the north to parts of Italy in the south. In addition, at the beginning of the Revolution, the ruler in Vienna was also known as the 'German' or Holy Roman Emperor. This meant that he received the allegiance of hundreds of states, statelets controlled by imperial knights or powerful clerics, and independent imperial cities. Napoleon's reorganisation of Germany in 1803 effectively destroyed the Holy Roman Empire and, in 1804, Emperor Francis took the title emperor of Austria. The final defeat of Napoleon did not restore the Holy Roman Empire (see Plate 17.3); it preserved the Austrian empire but this empire had shifted its focus. In 1789, the German empire, as the name suggested, covered much of Germany; in 1815, territorially the Austrian empire was far less 'German'.

On the eve of the French Revolution the empire had been ruled by Joseph II, a man fired with the ideas of the Enlightenment and keen to reform his territories along these lines. His reforms provoked considerable hostility. Joseph died and was succeeded by his brother, Leopold, at the beginning of 1790. Leopold's first task was to pacify the nobles, clergy and others incensed by Joseph's changes. There is some justification for believing that Leopold would have transformed the empire into a constitutional state but he died suddenly leaving the throne to his son, Francis, early in 1792. Francis, at 24 years of age, was a good example of the problems that could result from hereditary, absolutist monarchy. He was lacklustre, narrow-minded, shy and unimaginative. Concerned about the spread of French ideas and internal subversion from French revolutionary sympathisers, he made political policing and censorship ever more intrusive. He used conservative jurists to hold up legal reform and when a new law code was eventually promulgated in 1811, it studiously ignored ideas of natural rights and limitations on state power. At the same time, concessions were made to the nobility and the church. The former maintained their authority over their peasantry; civil equality was excluded from social relations in rural districts. The church maintained its influence in schooling. Military necessity required some attempts at fiscal improvement and reforms in the army, but when Napoleon defeated the Austrians again in 1809, the reformers were removed from office and the reforms went into reverse.

Following the defeat in 1809, Francis appointed Prince Clemens von Metternich as his principal minister. Metternich was conservative and his real strength lay in shrewd, pragmatic diplomacy. Initially, he appears to have hoped to stay in some sort of alliance with Napoleon, seeing the French emperor as a counterweight to Austria's other big neighbour, Russia. He swung to opposing Napoleon in 1813 when the deteriorating situation of the French, following the disastrous invasion of Russia, made it seem the sensible thing to do.

On balance, the Austrian imperial state survived the French wars with a changed geographic and ethnic structure, but little internal reorganisation. Being on the winning side, the empire's sheer size and its extremely able principal minister helped it to maintain the position of a great power. Influential states do not have to have extremely effective fiscal policies or particularly modern, efficient internal structures. For the first half of the nineteenth century, Austria was able to maintain supremacy in Germany, but thereafter it rapidly ceded this place to Prussia.

Prince Clemens von Metternich (1773–1859) was born and brought up in the Rhineland, where his father was the Austrian representative to several small states. He entered Austrian service himself at the close of the century, engaging in several diplomatic missions. Austrian ambassador to Berlin (1803) and Paris (1806), he became foreign minister in October 1809. He was cautious about opposing Napoleon in 1813 but eventually brought Austria into the war against him. He played a key role in the Congress of Vienna and dominated Germany after Napoleon's final defeat. Politically a conservative, his guiding principle was to maintain stability within Europe by a balance of power. ~ *DIPLOMACY* Associated with policies that were aimed at suppressing all liberal and revolutionary manifestations in Europe, he was forced to resign by the revolution in Vienna in 1848. He went briefly into exile in London and Brussels, returned to Austria in 1851 but never again held office.

The constitutional monarchy

The British state during the period presents a fascinating contrast. If the French empire was an example of an effective modernising centralised state with a written code promising equality and a relatively effective police institution guaranteeing security, and if the Austrian empire was an example of the persistence of the old regime – where is the British state best situated?

According to Jonathan Clark, at the end of the eighteenth and beginning of the nineteenth century Britain was an old regime state (Clark, 2000). Clark argues that too often historians of eighteenth-century Britain have concentrated on the emergence of those things that were to become central to nineteenth-century Britain – individualism, industry, liberalism and reform. This, he insists, has been at the expense of a true recognition of what Britain was like in the eighteenth century when it was, above all else, Anglican, aristocratic and monarchical. It was, he stresses, a confessional state, by which he means that a single faith was established in law to which a majority of the population were expected to conform. (You will remember, from Unit 12, that the Toleration Act gave religious dissenters freedom of worship but no civil rights.) The real change came at the end of the 1820s, when Anglican bishops failed to defend their faith sufficiently against the repeal of legislation limiting the rights of those subscribing to other Christian denominations.

Clark's reappraisal has provoked considerable debate and forced some rethinking of the political nature of British society in the eighteenth century. For the period of the revolutionary and Napoleonic wars, it is fair to say that the monarchy acquired a new importance and that the officer corps of the British army was recruited entirely from the gentry, if not necessarily 'aristocratic', and the men purchased their commissions (indeed, this remained the case throughout the nineteenth century). The officer ranks of the navy were also gentlemen, but nautical skill was of particular importance for promotion. To this extent, the old regime was perpetuated throughout the wars and beyond. Yet there are other elements of the British state as manifested in the period of the revolutionary and Napoleonic wars that suggest the need for some qualification of Clark's arguments and that, at best, muddy the waters for defining an 'old regime' state.

Among the hopes of the French monarchy when it called the estates general and precipitated revolution was a fiscal system that would balance the state's books and enable wars to be fought successfully. Among the aspirations of the early French revolutionaries were equality before the law, an end to the vestiges of seigniorial power and a degree of limitation on absolutist monarchical power. In eighteenth-century Britain, parliament could present a challenge to the monarch and his ministers, though the system was far from democratic and no parliamentarians spoke in terms of a 'sovereign people'. The gentry were extremely powerful, but they had no call on unpaid labour service from tenants or peasants. Englishmen took pride in their equality before the law and in their right to trial by jury. Encroachments on liberties during the war years, when there were fears of internal subversion and French

old regime?

New regime, according to previous page 16.

our revolution was earlier.

invasion, caused disquiet even among some of the MPs who advocated them. Finally, the fiscal system was among the most, if not the most, efficient in Europe. The British system of taxation and the government's ability to raise loans had been apparent throughout the eighteenth century. During the wars against revolutionary and Napoleonic France, Britain's credit-worthiness and fiscal strength enabled it to act as the paymaster and armaments supplier of every military coalition raised against the French.

The British state was not centralised and it did not seek to centralise. In England and Wales, and to a lesser extent in Scotland, local government was run by the gentry in their capacity as magistrates. They organised the administration that brought in the taxes and that filled county militia regiments. They organised the quotas demanded for the regular army and navy in 1795 and 1796, the nearest that Britain ever got to conscription during the wars. These men also served in parliament and were often the principal taxpayers. Reform of the fiscal system came at the end of the wars after poor auditing, poor command structures and the number of sinecures had been exposed by both political radicals and official enquiries. The system that had provided the finance for military victory was then dismantled, but by the very politicians who had profited from it.

In restoration France, the prefects notoriously failed to keep the electoral lists up to date and occasionally they sought to structure the lists to ensure the success of ministerial candidates. Yet the electoral system possessed a rational basis. Electors (all men) had to be aged 30 or more and to pay 300 francs in direct taxation; candidates had to be aged 40 or more and pay 1000 francs. The deputies to the assembly were renewed annually by one-fifth and were voted from departmental lists. In Britain, the electoral system had no rationality, except perhaps in the counties where, regardless of size, each county sent two members. Some boroughs had wide electorates; but others had no more than a dozen or so electors. And even when the electorate was large, an agreement between local politicians could mean that there was no contest. In 1818, in the first general election after Waterloo, for example, there were ballots in only six of the fourteen borough constituencies in Yorkshire and in only three of the six in Lancashire. It was another fourteen years before the Great Reform Act of 1832 introduced a consistency into the constituency structure and voting qualifications in the British state. Paradoxically, in so doing, the act disfranchised more working-class men than it enfranchised.

[handwritten margin note: "rotten boroughs"]

The military state

Look again at the maps (*Visual Sources*, Plates 17.1–17.3) and this time focus on the kingdom of Prussia. If Austria became less 'German' as a result of the Congress of Vienna, it might equally be argued that Prussia became more German with its acquisition of a major part of the Rhineland. But note also how, following on from its catastrophic defeats in 1805–06, Prussia was greatly reduced in size at the peak of Napoleon's power. A series of reforms between 1806 and 1812 enabled Prussia, while technically Napoleon's ally, to come back as a major player in European politics and a major contributor to Napoleon's final defeat.

Read Anthology Document 5.4, 'Riga memorandum, September 1807', which comprises extracts from Hardenberg's Riga memorandum.

1   What does Hardenberg consider that Prussia must do to survive?

2   What problems do you suppose could arise internally from introducing such a programme?

Spend about 10 minutes on this exercise.

1   Hardenberg is advocating root and branch reform here. What he is proposing are internal reforms not greatly different from those undertaken by the French in the early stages of their Revolution – freedom and equality (though not 'pure democracy'); opportunities for people to achieve to the best of their abilities, rather than being restricted by class or exclusive practices imposed on forms of employment and trade; opportunities for all to obtain property.

2   Such a reform programme would be likely to run into opposition from conservatives and vested interests whose privileges it would undermine.

Eighteenth-century Prussia was the smallest of Europe's 'great powers'. But it had a fearsome army and, in Frederick the Great (reigned 1740–86), a fearsome and very able monarch. Frederick's successors, however, were ordinary and his army atrophied under the command of elderly generals leading to the disastrous double battle of Jena-Auerstadt on 14 October 1806.

A group of enthusiastic reformers were available to Frederick William III in the aftermath of the defeats and some were already in his government. Notable among these was Karl Frieherr vom Stein, who came from an old family of imperial knights and who had been in Prussian service since 1780. Stein had ideas similar to those expressed in Hardenberg's memorandum, but unlike Hardenberg he was difficult and uncompromising. It is a mark of how serious the king considered Prussia's situation to be that, having dismissed Stein for insubordination in January 1807, he recalled him as chief minister the following October. Stein persuaded the king to replace his personal advisors with ministers responsible for formulating and executing the policies of ministries that were to be proper bureaucratic departments of state. He was responsible for an edict issued in October 1807 'On the facilitation of property ownership, the free use of land and the personal condition of the peasants' that set out to establish civil equality, economic freedom and a degree of social mobility. In November the following year, a new edict introduced elections and a degree of popular representation into local government.

These reforms provoked anger and resistance, especially among the noble landowners, the *Junkers*, but it was not they who forced Stein's removal from office in November 1808. Napoleon's agents intercepted documents which revealed that Stein was involved with individuals seeking a new war, and it was pressure from Paris that forced Frederick William's hand. The reforming policies were only temporarily impeded, however, since in June 1810 Hardenberg was appointed as head of the Prussian government. Hardenberg remained more flexible and responsive to pressure from the *Junkers* than Stein. Nevertheless, he succeeded in abolishing gild restrictions and tax exemptions and, by making peasants the free proprietors of two-thirds of their holdings (the remaining third went as compensation to the lord), he made significant moves towards the emancipation of the peasantry (finally achieved in 1816) *PRUSSIA* and towards the general freeing of labour. Those peasants with the smallest holdings, however, were the significant losers in these reforms: they become landless labourers.

Reforms of the Prussian state were not confined to civil society. The army also had its reformers. In 1808, August von Gneisnau, who had won considerable credit for his defence of the town of Colburg against the French in the previous year, wrote a memorandum reminiscent of that of Hardenberg:

> The Revolution aroused the full spectrum of energy and assigned each force to its proper sphere. This resulted in heroes being put at the head of the armies, statesmen being placed in charge of the leading administrative posts, and ultimately the greatest man of a great people reaching the top ... The Revolution set the full vigour of the French nation in motion. By giving equality to the several estates and by equitable taxation of property it transformed the living energy of man and the dead energy of goods into a proliferating pool of capital, upsetting the erstwhile relationships among states and the balance that rested on them. If the other states wish to restore that balance, they must mobilise and utilise the same resources.
>
> (Quoted in Ritter, 1972, p. 72)

Gneisnau was one of a group of officers who gathered around General Gerhard von Scharnhorst, who was appointed minister of war in 1808. Their reforms bore fruit in the German war of liberation (*Die Befreiungskrieg*) during which Prussia was able to field an army of 250,000 men, made up of regulars, volunteers and men from a new territorial force (*Landwehr*) based on universal military obligation. The numbers were roughly the same as those in the Austrian and Russian armies, but Prussia was considerably smaller and financially poorer than these two empires. The effort was phenomenal, incorporating perhaps 15 per cent of the adult male population of the truncated Prussia.

The Prussian nobility was happy to see an end to Napoleon but had no intention of taking the French route to change. In the aftermath of the war, the nobles resisted and reversed many of the changes, even in the army. They were assisted in this by the king's refusal to bring Stein back into government, by Scharnhorst's death from wounds following the battle of Lützen and by the fact that the reformers themselves had never constituted a united front. There were those who were content to go no further than limited reforms to free the economy and others who wanted to carry through reforms to release new energies. Moreover, after 1815 there was no longer the pressure of the state surviving under the Napoleonic onslaught. For the next generation, Prussia was prepared to be the junior partner to Metternich's Austria in maintaining political stability within the *Deutsche Bund*, the confederation that was established by the Congress of Vienna and that gave a loose organisation to all the German states.

THE VIEW FROM BELOW

The ministers and monarchs assembled at the Congress of Vienna were hostile to ideas of the sovereign people and of nations (see Anthology Document 5.9, 'Prince Metternich's political confession of faith, sent to Tsar Alexander I, December 1820'). Yet the Europe that emerged out of the revolutionary and Napoleonic wars was one in which nation states – that is, states built around a supposed single ethnicity on recognised national territory – came to dominate. Several theorists of the modern state and of nationalism have noted a step change in the concepts of nation and state from this period. In one of the earliest analyses of the idea of the modern nation, delivered in 1882, the French academic Ernest Renan, declared that: 'It is France's glory to have proclaimed, through the French Revolution, that a nation exists by itself ... The principle of nationhood is ours' (quoted in Woolf, 1996, p. 51).

[handwritten margin note: Unit definition]

But in addition to the nation in arms of 1792–93, *la grande nation* of the late 1790s and the imperial drive under Napoleon, historians have also pointed to the simultaneous emergence of nationalist sentiment in other countries and regions. This sentiment appears to have been inspired by the French example but at times also motivated by resistance to the French. In Germany, during the period of Napoleonic domination, a range of individuals from academics to soldiers urged popular resistance based on German-ness. The word *Befreiungskrieg* implied a national uprising against the French and it was used in this way by liberals, romantics and others urging some kind of German national unit beyond the *Bund* in the aftermath of the wars. There were those who aspired to Italian national unity in similar ways, though they could not point to a 'war of liberation' involving Italian armies. Insurrections against Napoleonic domination in Spain and the Tyrol have also been interpreted as manifestations of popular national sentiment.

EXERCISE

Looking back on what you have read in this unit so far:

1   What is there to support the idea of a significant development in national sentiment between 1792 and 1815?

2   What is there to suggest that such an idea needs some qualification?

Spend about 15 minutes on this exercise.

SPECIMEN ANSWER

1   The unit began with a rousing declaration and a rousing song, each based on the idea of the sovereign French people going to war against kings, aristocrats, tyrants and so forth for the benefit of humanity. It has also noted reformers outside France hoping to raise similar sentiments against the French.

2   The unit has also pointed to hostility among the French population towards conscription and reluctance among many European rulers to encourage national ideas among their populations for fear of where this might ultimately lead.

This leads on to the question of what people thought they were fighting for and what legacies the experience of war left across Europe with reference to ideas of state and nation.

The French experience

EXERCISE

What kinds of individuals were responsible for writing the texts in Anthology Documents 5.1 and 5.2 and would you say that they were typical of the population as a whole?

Spend about 5 minutes on this exercise.

SPECIMEN ANSWER

They were politicians and a poet. They were probably not typical of the population as a whole. Certainly the kind of language that they used was not that which tripped readily off the tongue of the majority.

Until the enormous interest in, and growth of, social history during the 1960s, few political historians were prepared to delve beyond this sort of language for assessing the development of ideas of nationalism. More recent research has stressed the view from below. The Marseilles battalion that marched into Paris in the summer of 1792, for example, sang their own words to the national anthem that took their name. These were rather more fruity and reflected the language of a youthful male-dominated barracks. But they also showed a critical (and arguably political) attitude to their enemies:

> March on, God's arse
> March on, God's fart
> The *émigrés*, by God
> Have no more idea of God
> Than old monarchist priests.
>
> (Quoted in Weber, 1976, p. 32)

Battle casualties, disease and desertion whittled down the mass army of 1793 so that, by the middle of the 1790s, when young generals like Napoleon were making their name, the French army was much less a reflection of a nation in arms than a smaller body of battle-hardened professionals. And while they may have sung typical squaddie songs, this army was also political, with the officers (many of whom had risen from the ranks) and the rank and file having beliefs drawn from militant Jacobinism. Bloody battles and new rounds of conscription in 1798 and then during the empire served to dilute much of this, which raises the question of how Napoleon inspired French soldiers and the French people in general.

↳ Azeglio on "making Italians" — top down philosophies.

EXERCISE

Read Anthology Document 5.5, 'Letters of Napoleon Bonaparte'.

1   What is Napoleon seeking to do here?

2   What word would we use to describe it?

3   Looking at Anthology Document 5.5(a), is there anything that strikes you as significant about the regions in which he wants the action focused?

Spend about 15 minutes on this exercise.

SPECIMEN ANSWER

1   He is seeking to use the press to portray his enemies in a bad light and to emphasise, by implication, his more principled behaviour and his own glory.

2   Propaganda; we might also use the words 'political spin'.

3   Brittany and the Vendée were areas of resistance to the revolutionary state and this resistance was inspired, in part, by hostility to the religious policies of the Revolution. Belgium and Piedmont were regions only recently incorporated into France.

DISCUSSION

In answer to the third question, I could also add that there had been a serious insurrection against French rule in Belgium that had some similarities with the uprisings in western France; and Napoleon was always suspicious of the Baroque Catholicism to be found across much of Italy, but I would not expect you to have known this.

Napoleon was an extremely effective propagandist. From the beginning of his career he was careful how he, and his activities, were portrayed. While he was commander of the French revolutionary army in Italy in 1796 and 1797, he had newspapers printed and circulated in France that stressed his own honest and noble attributes and played up the undoubted successes of his army. As emperor, he issued army bulletins that were similar. There was a popular saying 'to lie like a bulletin'. Yet even if people (and especially his veterans) knew to take them with a very large pinch of salt, the bulletins had a knack of saying what people wanted to believe – one last effort would bring total victory; Napoleon would bring them through. There was nothing abstract in the bulletins and other written elements of Napoleon's propaganda, unlike the high-flown documents of the revolutionaries. The army bulletins in particular possessed a personal and immediate quality; Napoleon's cause was his men's cause, his glory was their glory. This was not a sovereign people at war; it was Napoleon's people and, particularly, Napoleon's men.

The revolutionaries had wondered how best to portray the sovereign people as a popular image. They experimented with Hercules (see Figure 17.1) and the female representation of liberty, who was also metamorphosed into Marianne, the personification of the French motherland (see Figure 17.2). Napoleon had no interest in the portrayal of the sovereign people, but he took a very close interest in the visual representations of Napoleon (see *Visual Sources*, Plates 17.4–17.6).

Many people in the provinces could pick up the messages of the written word but were unlikely to see, let alone have the ability to decode, the carefully

Rév. de Paris.   Le Peuple mangeur de Rois.   Nº. 217. P. 290.

Statue Colossale proposée par le journal des Révolutions de Paris pour être placée sur les points les plus éminens de nos frontières.

Figure 17.1 'Le peuple mangeur de rois' (the people, eater of kings), engraving. Musée Carnavalet, Paris. Photo: © Photothèque des Musées de la Ville de Paris / Cliché: Andreani. An illustration of the people as Hercules drawn for the revolutionary newspaper *Révolutions de Paris*. In the period of Jacobin ascendancy in 1793–94, the Greek god Hercules was appropriated as a revolutionary figure. Here, wearing the Phrygian cap of the revolutionaries, he roasts a king in front of a heavily defended fortress from which fly the tricolour banners of revolutionary France

constructed images of either the Hercules/sovereign people or Napoleon. Conscription remained an irritant, but it appears that, as the people grew more and more accustomed to the annual levies and the certainties of the state's unpleasantness if they resisted, so conscription began to be accepted as a fact of life, albeit an unpleasant one. Moreover, the Napoleonic state was reasonably popular as long as the people did not feel threatened and as long as the empire was being successfully used to keep the French people fed and in work. A particularly bad harvest in 1811 provoked unrest over the high cost of bread. The increased levies of men following the Russian disaster and the advance of the allied armies also provoked discontent (see Figure 17.3). Yet there is some ambiguity here. The threat of invasion by Anglo-Spanish troops from the south-west and by Russians and Germans from the north-east conceivably sparked some of the old sentiments of 1792–93. Napoleon's campaign on the north-east frontier in 1813–14 with a largely untried conscript army was one of his most brilliant, even if he was forced to retreat and then forced to abdicate by military commanders who had had enough. During his last gamble in 1815, 'La Marseillaise', the fierce battle hymn of 1792, was

Figure 17.2 Liberty or Marianne as the official vignette of the Executive Directory, 1798 (the regime that ran France from November 1795 to November 1799, when it was overthrown by Napoleon's coup). Bibliothèque Nationale, Paris, Collection De Vinck 6584. Photo: Bibliothèque Nationale de France. Again Liberty wears the Phrygian cap, her arm rests on the Constitution of Year III of the Republic. To one side of this is the Gallic cock. During the Jacobin period she was often shown armed with a pike

Le Minotaure, Corse

Figure 17.3 The Corsican Minotaur, cartoon. Bibliothèque Nationale, Paris, Cabinet des Estampes, Hennin 13261. Photo: Bibliothèque Nationale de France. Strict censorship meant that it was rare for cartoons and caricatures to appear critical of Napoleon. This dates from 1814. It shows the Archchancellor of the empire, Jean-Jacques-Régis Cambacérès (1753–1824) – 'the second most important man in Napoleonic France' (Woloch, 2001, p. 120) – feeding Napoleon with plates of conscripts. Napoleon, in turn, defecates kings

played again after a long silence (and I don't know what version of the words the army sang in 1815).

Read Anthology Document 5.6, 'Reflections of a romantic'.

1   What sort of document is this?

2   In what way is it looking back on the Napoleonic adventure?

Spend about 10 minutes on this exercise.

1   It is a literary reflection on the events of Napoleon's reign. In a sense it is autobiographical. De Musset was in his fifth year when Napoleon was finally defeated at Waterloo.

2   It looks back with nostalgia. De Musset feels that he and his generation have missed out on the great adventure. They were born during war, but have never left their home towns, and certainly not as soldiers.

You might have a certain amount of difficulty empathising with De Musset's longings, yet he was not alone in such sentiments. A clutch of young romantics wrote similarly; the heroes of Stendhal's greatest novels *Le rouge et le noir* (1830) and *La chartreuse de Palme* (1839) are both young romantics who feel that their futures have been blighted by Napoleon's defeat. Romantic artists and poets continued to glamorise and glorify aspects of the imperial and revolutionary past; though this had to be done with care during the restoration. There were the men in government employment who believed that they were passed over or dismissed because they had been loyal to the emperor on his return in 1815. And then there were others who were relieved to see a quarter of a century of wars and internal upheaval at an end.

Twenty-five years of revolution and war had left the French state with a much more efficient administrative structure than that which had been overthrown in 1789. But above the solid administrative machine, politics could be coloured by positions adopted during the Revolution or under Napoleon. Under the restoration, both old Jacobins and Bonapartists were in opposition; the former were radicals, the latter claimed to be liberals. Both could appeal to the sovereign people when it suited them and use their own interpretations of history to demonstrate the legitimacy of such appeals. Problems arose for governments when they united this opposition and through political misjudgement, or as a result of economic misfortune, enabled it to become the voice of the majority, resurrecting the appeal of the sovereign people against monarchical 'tyranny'. Fifteen years after Waterloo, this was the fate of Charles X. In the 'three glorious days' of the July Revolution, the people of Paris overthrew the Bourbon monarchy and replaced it with a cadet branch of the family, the house of Orleans. The new king, Louis Philippe, took the title 'king of the French' rather than 'king of France'; he also became known as 'the citizen king'. After the Revolution of 1830 there was a purge. Of the eighty-six prefects, only three remained in the posts; another four were transferred but seventy-nine were simply dismissed. The purge even spread down to local mayors. A high percentage of the replacements were men who had served during the empire, some of whom had even refused to work under the restored Bourbons. But the 'replacements' came from the same social group as their predecessors. The fundamental administrative structure of France was left unchanged and continued looking very largely as it had emerged from the Napoleonic period.

Continental Europe

I have stressed the wariness that European monarchs and ministers felt towards raising nations in arms. Yet, in March 1813, Frederick William III urged his people (*Mein Volk*) to remember their heroic ancestors, the Russians and Spaniards who had risen against the French, and to rise up themselves as 'Prussians and Germans' (see Anthology Document 5.7). And, as noted above, the Prussians put an enormous percentage of their population in the field. What did they think they were fighting for?

The core of the Prussian army in 1813–14 was a rump of regulars from the old army defeated in 1806–07. Napoleon had insisted that the Prussian army be reduced in size and this meant that only those interested in a professional military career stayed on. The conscripts of 1813 were clustered around these professionals. The depredations of the remnant of the imperial army that had escaped the Russian debacle provoked some populist guerrilla activity and probably encouraged many to come forward when the levies were made in 1813. Possibly few of the conscripts thought that they would be fighting far from home. Volunteers also came forward and these were especially important in the subsequent mythology of the *Befreiungskrieg*. In fact, most of these came forward after universal conscription was announced and many of them probably volunteered as it was a way of avoiding conscription. Volunteers had to supply their own equipment and their own officers. This was popular with townsmen as it meant that they did not have to serve alongside peasants and labourers or take orders from noble officers. It foreshadowed the later Prussian practice of permitting educated men to serve for one rather than three years in the regular army. It also confirmed prevailing social attitudes and relationships rather than challenging them. The new army of 1813 was quickly marched into battle and quickly set off after the withdrawing French. Men on the move in alien land tended to stick with their comrades and found it more difficult to desert and walk home.

Three final points about the enormous Prussian effort of 1813–14 are worth contrasting with the French experience. First, the conflict was over fairly rapidly. Within a year of the major mobilisation, Napoleon had abdicated for the first time. Second, the Prussian economy never had to put itself on a war footing like the French. There was no need to make arms and ammunition. Once the Prussians (and the Austrians) had committed themselves against Napoleon, the Baltic ports were bursting with munitions supplied by the British. Finally, as may be apparent from the brief discussion of the conscripts and volunteers, and the cold-shouldering of reformers like Stein, for all its massive military commitment, the Prussian elite never yielded its position to any notions of popular sovereignty.

The liberals and romantics of the postwar period, however, tended to read the events of the *Befreiungskrieg* rather differently. They stressed the German-ness of the war: patriotic leaders like Adolf Freiherr von Lützow who had led a unit of volunteers in the German colours of black, red and gold; and romantic young volunteers like the poet Theodor Körner who, before his death in a skirmish near Mecklenburg, had penned verses about German brothers united by God, blood and the belief in the fatherland. The memory of the war and of these romantic heroes fuelled the calls for German unification. But Germany was not to be united until more than half a century after Waterloo – and then it was as an empire encompassing several kingdoms under Prussian dominance, rather than as a separate, single nation state.

The Tyrol never became a separate country or a nation state. At the beginning of the nineteenth century it was a largely autonomous rural province of the Habsburgs; indeed it had been a Habsburg province since the fourteenth century. Its population was largely peasant and deeply religious. It had resisted the Enlightenment reforms of Emperor Joseph II and its resistance to Enlightenment ideas took on a counter-revolutionary element when men from the Tyrol fought the armies of the French Revolution during the 1790s. After his victory at Austerlitz in 1805, Napoleon separated Tyrol from Austria and handed it to his ally, Maximilian I Joseph of Bavaria. The Bavarians were Catholic themselves, but Maximilian I Joseph's regime shared the Enlightenment suspicion of the extravagant manifestations of religion that were found among the Tyrolese. They banned the Midnight Mass celebration at Christmas, weather prayers and field processions. They also raised taxes. Tyrolean patriots negotiated with the court in Vienna promising an uprising against their new masters that would coincide with the renewed Austrian challenge to Napoleon in 1809. In the event, the Tyrolese, under the command of a rural innkeeper, Andreas Hofer, proved rather more formidable than the Austrians. The defeat of the Austrians also left them on their own. Even so, Napoleon had to authorise the despatch of imperial troops from Italy to assist the Bavarians in suppressing the revolt. Hofer was captured, taken to Mantua and shot.

The Tyrolean uprising was short lived, from the spring to the autumn of 1809. It was fought to maintain the province's old privileges, its traditional form of Catholicism and its hostility to Protestants and Jews. But the memory of what became known as *Anno Neun* (year nine) remained potent, especially when the tide turned against Napoleon in 1813–14. It became rather more difficult to praise popular insurrection, no matter how conservative in aim, in the early period of the restoration. But in 1823, officers of one of the crack units of the Austrian army, the *Tiroler Kaiserjäger*, marching home through Mantua decided to take Hofer's body with them. The Austrian government was not enthusiastic but it eventually agreed to Hofer's remains being interred in one of the principal churches of the Tyrolean capital, Innsbruck. *Anno Neun* and the *Heldenjahr* (heroes' year) became popular subjects for plays, poems, songs and other cultural artefacts in the Tyrol. They did not figure greatly in the broader culture of the multi-ethnic Austrian empire, not least because of the implication that the Austrians had betrayed the Tyrolese by ceding their lands to Bavaria a second time and while they were still fighting. Some nineteenth-century German national historians (though naturally not those from Bavaria) also claimed Hofer and his fighters as precursors of the *Befreiungskrieg*.

The best-known popular insurrection against Napoleon, however, was that in Spain from 1808 to 1814. Recent detailed research into the events, however, has challenged the extent to which Napoleon's 'Spanish ulcer' is best described as a popular or people's war. In May 1808, the people of Madrid rose against a French army in their city and similar uprisings occurred elsewhere over the next few weeks. These were genuinely popular, and that of Madrid occurred even before Napoleon had compelled the king of Spain and his heir to renounce the throne. Over the next five years or so, the fighting in Spain was a chaotic mixture of conventional war, involving Spanish regular armies and a British army ranged against the French, and savage guerrilla conflict. Some of the guerrillas were eventually organised into significant bands acting in conjunction with the regular Spanish and British armies; but others were scarcely distinguishable from bandit gangs and were as much a threat to the native population as they were to the French.

The Spanish elite divided between traditionalists, liberals opposed to Napoleon and progressive reformers who backed the kinds of changes introduced by the French. The liberals dominated the Cortez (a national assembly) that met in Cadiz in 1812 and promulgated a constitution that established a uniform legal code and freedom of the press. They still maintained Catholicism as the state religion, but they abolished the Inquisition. The final ejection of the French brought the uncompromising Ferdinand VII to the throne. He promptly abolished the new constitution and persecuted the liberals. By surrounding himself with noble favourites, few of whom had done anything in the war, he also succeeded in alienating many loyal army officers, and this provoked a series of military coups. The most serious and successful of these in 1820 compelled Ferdinand to reintroduce the constitution of 1812; but continuing unrest prompted a French invasion, which restored Ferdinand to full power once again.

While Spain emerged from the revolutionary and Napoleonic period with a reactionary monarch, a powerful Catholic Church and an army that, periodically, considered it had the right to take action to hold the country together or uphold the generals' interpretation of what was best for the state, the memory of the popular uprisings and the guerrillas was also important. Even in restoration Spain the people were recognised as a political presence. As a recent historian of the guerrilla conflict has concluded:

> whatever politicians and generals might think of them in private, [the people] were now a force to which it was necessary to pay lip service and to whom competing political movements could appeal for

legitimacy. Even before the war had ended the liberals had set themselves up as veritable tribunes of the people, whilst after 1814 it was a key part of the absolutist case that their enemies had usurped the people's sovereignty and governed in despite of the popular will rather than in accordance with its dictates.

(Esdaile, 2004, p. 204)

'The bonny bunch of roses'

Sometime in the aftermath of the Napoleonic wars, an unknown British balladeer wrote 'The bonny bunch of roses'. The ballad describes a meeting on a seashore between Napoleon's son ('Napoleon II', properly the duke of Reichstadt) and his mother (Marie-Louise of Austria). Marie-Louise sings of Napoleon's lonely exile on the south Atlantic island of St Helena. The tone is sympathetic to Napoleon but it is also patriotic: Napoleon was defeated because he failed to beware of the bonny bunch of roses – England, Ireland and Scotland – whose unity cannot be broken.

I have already noted Britain's key role in the wars; indeed Britain's conflict with revolutionary and Napoleonic France brought an end to a century of sporadic fighting ('the second hundred years war' as it has been characterised) that began during the reigns of Louis XIV and William of Orange. The eighteenth-century wars had been fought all over the globe – in America, India and, especially, in the profitable sugar islands of the West Indies. There was an element of ideological hostility to the wars. Britain appeared as a model constitutional state, France as a model absolutist one. The British state was staunchly Protestant; the French were Catholic. The rivalries re-emerged during the 1790s. There were significant members of the British government and among the commercial elite who saw the wars as an opportunity for winning the commercial war in the West Indies (see Figure 17.4). The Protestant/Catholic confrontation was now replaced with what many saw as a clash between Christianity and an atheist, levelling ideology characterised as Jacobinism. Some British conservatives wished to see the restoration of the Bourbon monarchy; others took a more pragmatic line and felt that, once France was contained, it scarcely mattered who was in charge. Those beneath the ruling elite had a traditional xenophobic attitude towards the French. British victories and national heroes, most notably Nelson, brought people onto the streets in massive, patriotic demonstrations (see Figure 17.5). When French invasion threatened, men enlisted in volunteer units to defend their homes (see Anthology Document 5.8, 'British volunteer forces called to arms'). Though, as was noted above in the case of Prussia in 1813, some men joined the volunteers to avoid ballots for the militia. Ballots for the militia, specified military and naval quotas that were required of towns and counties in 1795 and 1796, and press gangs infuriated people and could provoke rioting. The disruption of the economy by the demands and pressures of war and by war taxes also led to unrest and dissatisfaction.

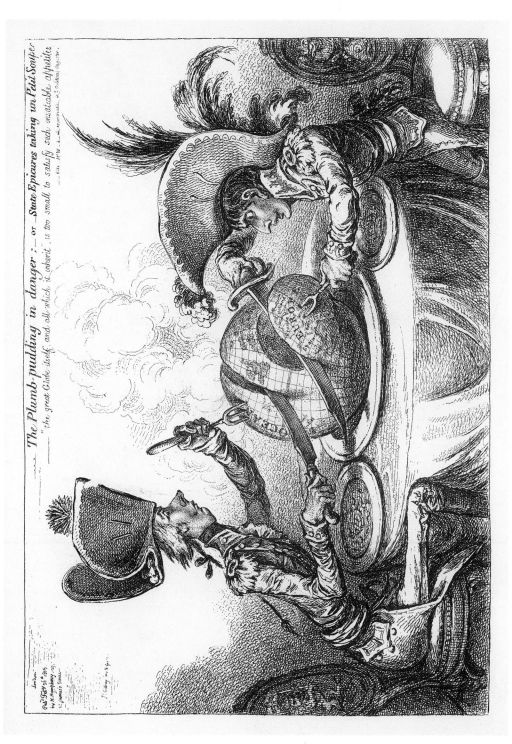

Figure 17.4 'The Plumb-pudding in danger; —or — State Epicures taking un Petit Souper', 26 February 1805, engraving. Photo: Mary Evans Picture Library. One of the most famous caricatures of James Gillray (1756–1815). Little Boney, as Gillray termed him, slices away at Europe with sword and fork while William Pitt, the younger, the British prime minister, uses a knife and Neptune's trident to acquire nearly half of the world/pudding. The quotation in the caption at the top right ('the great globe itself, and all which it inherit is too small to satisfy such insatiable appetites') although attributed to the politician William Windham seems to be based rather on a quotation from Shakespeare's *The Tempest*

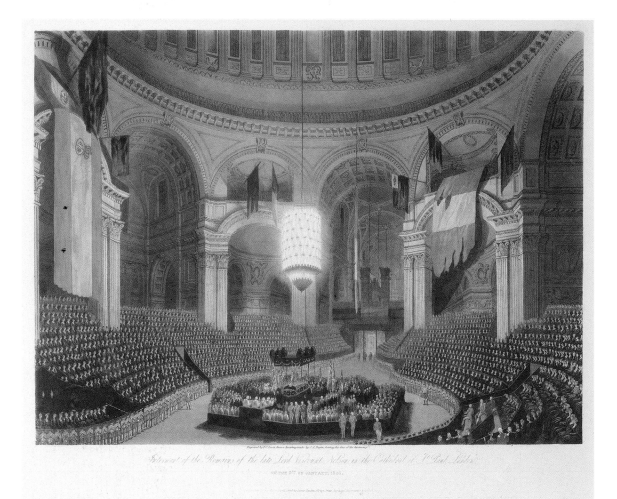

Figure 17.5 'Interment of the Remains of the late Lord Nelson in the Cathedral of St Paul, London, on the 9th of January 1806'. Engraved by F.C. Lewis from a drawing made by C.A. Pugin, during the time of the ceremony. © National Maritime Museum, London. Military victories became the opportunities for great celebrations during the revolutionary and Napoleonic wars. Anyone who dared not to illuminate their windows during such a celebration was likely to have their house attacked and windows broken by angry crowds. By the same token, Nelson's death at Trafalgar and his funeral were the occasions of great outpourings of national grief. His funeral cortege, up the Thames from Greenwich, and the funeral itself in St Paul's were massive events watched by thousands. The image here shows the raked seating constructed in the cathedral under tattered flags taken from French and Spanish ships at Trafalgar. Such a funeral for a commoner, with the king and ministers among the mourners, was unprecedented

---

EXERCISE

Read Anthology Document 5.10, 'A soldier and a citizen', which is an extract from William Cobbett's *Advice to Young Men*'.

1   Note down what you take to be the key point of Cobbett's argument.

2   How far had the revolutionary and Napoleonic wars achieved that for which Cobbett was arguing?

Spend about 15 minutes on this exercise.

1   Cobbett's argument is straightforward: if a man is expected to fight for his country, then he should have a say in the running of the country.

2   The wars had not led to any change in the constitutional structure. (See the brief discussion above in the section on 'The constitutional monarchy'.)

Cobbett was an active radical during the war years and the kinds of arguments raised here were also raised then. At the same time, some members of the British ruling elite expressed the kinds of concerns that have already been described in Austria and Prussia – what would be the impact of using French ways to beat the French?

Overall, Linda Colley has concluded that the period of the revolutionary and Napoleonic wars, building on a century of conflict against France, was central in the invention of the British nation. She describes a national awareness, already emerging in eighteenth-century ideas of a freedom-loving Protestant nation, cohering around the monarchy, heightened by resistance to invasion and, ultimately, by the celebration of victory (Colley, 1992). John Cookson has acknowledged the force of her argument, but he has also proposed some reassessment. He puts a greater emphasis of the opportunistic, interested and conditional patriotism of the poorer classes who came forward, for instance, as volunteers. He also stresses the 'three kingdoms', the bonny bunch of roses of England, Scotland (united with England in 1707) and Ireland (united with the British crown in 1800) and their distinct attitudes and responses. The Scots and the Irish appear to have had disproportionate numbers of men in the armed services in comparison with the English. Their memory of participation was also different. Scots' participation helped boost a martial image for the Scot within the Anglo-Scottish union, which was maintained throughout the nineteenth century. The Irish had some difficulty with martial memory of the wars. For much of the nineteenth century, most Catholic Irish sentiment remained broadly loyal to the crown; most had no wish to draw attention to the 'wild geese' who fought for France or to the defeated insurrections of 1798 and 1801. The Protestant Irish, similarly, had no wish to encourage any Catholic pretensions. Unlike the martial nature emphasised in Scottish identity, the nineteenth-century Irish tended to stress identity based on a distinctive culture (Cookson, 1997).

CONCLUSION

This unit has ranged far and wide across Europe over a long period. I want to get you to draw it together now in your own mind by thinking about what I consider to be the main issues that have been touched on, primarily with reference to the state and state formation.

1   What was the key shift in the individual's relationship to the state emanating from the French Revolution?

2   How far did these ideas spread across Europe in the period under consideration?

[Handwritten annotations in left margin:]
[SUBJECT]
serfdom –
the "monarchical state"

[Box:] SPECIMEN ANSWER
Thru "revolutionary state"
to
a "nation state"
[CITIZEN]

3   What changes discussed above show the state in this period becoming more far-reaching and efficient?

4   Is there a new role for nation and nationalism in these new states? (This is a tricky one.)

Spend about 20 minutes on this exercise.

1   Revolutionary declarations and legislation identified the citizen (admittedly the *male* citizen) as a member of the nation and the state, not simply the *subject* of a prince. Citizens were part of the sovereign people in whom authority ultimately existed – of course, things did not work out quite like this in practice, but that was a new and very potent and significant idea.

2   The Revolution was exceptional and, even when they needed popular support for fighting wars and appealed to 'their people', the princes of Europe were generally opposed to engaging far with such ideas.

3   The organisation for, and fighting of, war had been a major preoccupation (perhaps even *the* major preoccupation) of the old regime state – but the new state, as typified by that of the French Revolution and Napoleon, was much more efficient and effective in marshalling the necessary men and money. This is illustrated by the long stretch of Napoleon's police force, and by his training system for senior state administrators through the recruitment of *auditeurs*.

4   Some historians and social scientists have identified the period of the French Revolution as seeing the birth of modern nationalism and the modern nation state. The idea of a *sovereign people* fighting for their *great nation* suggests a significant development in such ideas. But there were also people who had no interest in fighting for their nation, or whose motivation looks to be, at least in part, self-interest. Moreover, it is difficult always to see Spanish bandits as heroic patriots. Can we call the Tyrolean fighters members of a 'nation'? And if the Germans fought a 'war of liberation', they fought it in the uniforms of Prussians, Bavarians, Württembergers and others, not in a *German* uniform, and their leaders had little concept at this time of a united German nation state.

REFERENCES

Brown, H.G. (1997) 'From organic state to security state: the war on brigandage in France, 1797–1802', *Journal of Modern History*, vol. 69, pp. 661–95.

Clark, J.C.D. (2000) *English Society, 1688–1832: Religion, Ideology and Politics During the Ancien Régime*, 2nd edn, Cambridge, Cambridge University Press.

Colley, L. (1992) *Britons: Forging the Nation, 1701–1837*, New Haven, London, Yale University Press.

Cookson, J.E. (1997) *The British Armed Nation, 1793–1815*, Oxford, Clarendon Press.

Emsley, C. (1988) 'Nationalist rhetoric and nationalist sentiment in revolutionary France' in Dann, O. and Dinwiddy, J. (eds) *Nationalism in the Age of the French Revolution*, London, Hambledon.

Esdaile, C.J. (2004) *Fighting Napoleon: Guerrillas, Bandits and Adventurers in Spain, 1808–1814*, New Haven, London, Yale University Press.

Ritter, G. (1972) *The Sword and the Sceptre: The Problem of Militarism in Germany*, vol. 1, *The Prussian Tradition 1740–1890*, London, Allen Lane.

Weber, E. (1976) 'Who sang the Marseillaise?' in Beauroy, J., Bertand, M. and Gargan, E.T. (eds) *The Wolf and the Lamb: Popular Culture in France from the Old Régime to the Twentieth Century*, Saratoga, Anma Libri.

Woloch, I. (2001) *Napoleon and his Collaborators: The Making of a Dictatorship*, New York, W.W. Norton.

Woolf, S. (1996) *Nationalism in Europe, 1815 to the Present: A Reader*, London, Routledge.

Clive Emsley

THE REVOLT OF THE SILESIAN WEAVERS, JUNE 1844

Once again, I want to start a unit by getting you to read a document and to answer some questions based on that reading. Anthology Document 5.11, 'The Silesian weavers' rising, June 1844', is a contemporary account of an incident in Silesia in 1844. Silesia was then a province of Prussia; it is now part of Poland. Read the document, thinking about the following questions.

1   Who wrote the account and when?

2   What credence do you give to the document? Would any different sort of account be more reliable?

3   What is given as the cause of the weavers' revolt?

4   What form did the revolt take?

Spend about 20 minutes on this exercise.

1   The author, Wolff, was a committed radical activist. He wrote this account almost immediately after the events described, but he was not an eye-witness himself.

2   Given the author's radical affiliations, it is reasonable to wonder whether he was overemphasising the plight of the weavers, the oppression of the employers and the violence of the authorities. It is also difficult to know just how far we can accept his account since he was not a witness. But then different sorts of account might not be much better. An account by an employer or by a military commander might be equally biased from the other side. A newspaper report would not be any less biased than Wolff and it would very probably have to depend on the testimony of witnesses given to a journalist – in other words, an origin much like this account. These problems are inherent in any historical research, but perhaps especially in that looking at protest and popular disorder.

More than one source.

3   General distress and low wages.

4   Briefly, crowds of weavers attacked the houses of manufacturers demanding better pay and presents. [I don't expect you to have noted this but it was common in such popular rebellions for the rioters to demand some 'payment' for their turbulent efforts; and such payment could also be taken as a sign of the victim's good faith over any promises exacted from him] The crowds treated different kinds of employer in different ways. The police were too thin on the ground to cope and the army was brought in. During a confrontation that developed as a crowd was lined up to receive some payment the troops opened fire, killing eleven people instantly and wounding others.

The revolt of the Silesian weavers became a frightening symbol for many in Prussian society (and in Germany more generally) of the shape of things that might come with the changing structure of the economy. The incident was taken up by a number of painters, novelists and poets. Most notable among the latter was Heinrich Heine, who wrote a searing critique of the events called simply 'The Silesian Weavers' (*Die schlesischen Weber*).

Silesia was a centre of linen production. The industry had been protected during the eighteenth century. Productivity had been high; the product was good quality and sold well, both in the home market and abroad. But in the early nineteenth century, and particularly when the Napoleonic wars were brought to an end, the industry began to be undermined from two directions. First, hand-loomed linen from Belgium and Ireland began to penetrate Germany and was cheaper; so too was machine-loomed linen from England. Even more of a threat to Silesian linen, however, was the growth of cotton manufacture, again largely from abroad. Some Silesian weavers and manufacturers tried switching to cotton (you will note that cotton is the textile mentioned in Wolff's account). But they could not compete with the prices of factory-produced British goods. Finally, the situation in Silesia was aggravated by a food crisis. Potatoes were the staple food of many weavers' families and in 1842 the harvest had been very poor, leading to malnutrition, disease and starvation.

There are several issues raised here that are commonly associated with nineteenth-century industrialisation: impoverished workers affected by new manufactures; direct action; possible class conflict. All of these will be explored in more detail in this unit. When you have successfully completed it you will have acquired sufficient knowledge to enable you to engage with questions concerning:

- the impact of economic changes on producers and consumers
- the inter-relationship between early nineteenth-century economic change and shifting beliefs and ideologies.

You will also have developed further your ability to:

- analyse historical documents
- think critically about historical issues

OTHER EXPERIENCES

Shortly after the events in Silesia, the young Karl Marx argued, more in hope than with his usual careful analysis, I think, that the weavers were starting where French and English workers finished:

> namely with an understanding of the nature of the proletariat. This *superiority* stamps the whole episode. Not only were machines destroyed, those competitors of the workers, but also the *account books*, the titles of ownership, and whereas all other movements had directed their attacks at the visible enemy, namely the *industrialists*, the Silesia workers also turned against the hidden enemy, the bankers. Finally, not one English workers' uprising was carried out with such courage, foresight and endurance.
>
> (Marx, 1975 [1844], p. 415)

The Silesian weavers were a group of producers under pressure from a variety of changes affecting their industry. Their plight was one that appears fairly common in popular interpretations of the development of industry in the early nineteenth century. But just how common was that experience? Did all industrial producers suffer? What of other kinds of producer, not just those engaged in industrial production but agricultural workers? And were not producers also consumers? Marx suggests in the passage quoted above that these workers were beginning to understand their identity as 'proletarians'. Assuming that to be true (and many would challenge the claim), the question then arises – how far was the identity of these producers being coloured by the new ideas of citizenship and sovereignty that spread across Europe with the French Revolution and the ensuing wars?

Karl Marx (1818–1883) was born in the Rhineland, the son of a Jewish lawyer who converted to Christianity in 1824. He studied history, law and philosophy at the universities of Bonn and Berlin. In 1842, he joined the staff of a radical newspaper, the *Rheinische Zeitung*, becoming an editor in the same year. He travelled to Paris, where he met his lifelong collaborator **Frederick Engels** (1820–1895), and became deeply involved with socialist thought and politics. Back in Germany in 1847, he and Engels wrote the *Communist Manifesto* (*Manifest der Kommunisten*). Tried for his political activities in 1849, he was acquitted. He moved first to Paris, then to London, where he remained for the rest of his life, developing his critique of the new society and working with working-class radicals, most notably the International Working Men's Association (established 1874).

British and French workers

In England during the closing years of the Napoleonic wars and the first years of peace, workers in a variety of textile industries had smashed machinery. The Luddites are commonly perceived as resisting the introduction of new machinery. In fact, their protest was more complex and it varied from trade to trade. In Nottinghamshire and the Midlands, Luddites were largely stocking weavers. These men often worked handlooms in their own homes. They protested principally against new pay rates and other devices introduced by certain employers to change their work regime and traditional patterns of payment. The machines that were smashed in the Midlands, stocking frames, were an Elizabethan invention. In the West Riding, in contrast, Luddism was directed against new machinery. The new shearing frames and gig mills threatened the livelihood of skilled croppers in the wool trade. In Lancashire, there were attacks on cotton mills operating new power looms. But here there were also threats against manufacturers who were employing cheap female (as opposed to the usual male) labour in the new factories. The situation was aggravated by high prices and food shortages; bread was a key component of the diet of the English working class and the harvest of 1812 was poor, as were those in the years immediately following the war with France. For the government, finding grain overseas to fill the gaps in the harvest in the midst of war was difficult and was made more so by Napoleon's attempt to blockade Britain. At the end of the wars, the British parliament introduced legislation to protect British agriculture. The Corn Laws were seen as keeping prices artificially high and they continued to generate discontent long after Luddism as such had disappeared. Finally, there was a political element to Luddism, especially in Lancashire, where the protesters adopted, on some occasions, the language of revolutionary radicalism akin to that of revolutionary France.

There were other violent economic protests by British industrial workers in the decades following Waterloo. Most of these were confined to particular trades and were localised. They usually accompanied strike action and there was a wave of violence when, in 1824, in a period of economic boom, parliament repealed the Combination Acts that had restricted trade union activity. Much more serious, in the summer of 1831, the workers of Merthyr Tydfil rose in revolt and were suppressed by military intervention. Merthyr was a boom town that had grown enormously over the preceding half century and was dominated by the iron industry. Wages in the town were higher than those in rural Wales, but there was instability in the iron trade, aggravated by a slump at the end of the 1820s. Cuts in the wages of miners and the dismissal of some ironworkers sparked the trouble. Political excitement and agitation for the Parliamentary Reform Bill then before parliament fanned the flames. Eight years later, during the first great wave of agitation for the People's Charter, South Wales miners again fought a bloody battle with troops, this time in Newport, Monmouthshire (see Figure 18.1). In 1842, across the northern counties, Chartism fused with protests over wage cuts into the 'plug plot', so called because activists brought factories to a halt by drawing the plugs of the boilers that drove the machinery.

These British demonstrations could be widespread across different parts of the country; they sometimes involved people whose working lives were being reshaped by factory labour. But by far the largest workers' uprisings of the period occurred in France in the city of Lyon, in the traditional luxury industry of silk weaving. Around 1830, roughly a quarter of the 180,000 people who lived in the city and its suburbs were involved in silk and silk-related trades. The industry was structured in a traditional manner. At the centre were the masters. These negotiated orders with merchants; they worked their own looms and employed journeymen to work on others. But there was a growing division between the masters. The overwhelming majority of them owned fewer than four looms and it was becoming increasingly difficult for the journeymen who worked on the extra looms ever to consider becoming masters themselves. Those masters who owned more than four looms were increasingly setting themselves apart; they lived in different districts and frequented different *cabarets* ('pubs' is not an exact translation, but it is, perhaps, the best there is). Yet, in spite of the emerging splits among the craftsmen, it was the merchants who were generally blamed for problems in the industry, particularly for offering low prices for woven silk. They were also condemned for attempts to undercut the weavers in the city by increasingly employing part-time rural

Figure 18.1 The battle of the Westgate Hotel, Newport, Monmouth, 4 November 1839. Photo: By permission of Llyfrgell Genedlaethol Cymru / The National Library of Wales. This is one of several popular prints made in the immediate aftermath of the clash between armed coalminer Chartists and men from the 45th Foot. Twenty miners were killed and some 125 individuals were subsequently brought before the courts; three were sentenced to death for treason, though the sentence was commuted to transportation.

labour. On two occasions, in November 1831 and in April 1834, the Lyon silk weavers rose in armed insurrection, allegedly fighting under a banner inscribed with *vivre en travaillant ou mourir en combattant* (to live working or to die fighting). Both insurrections were tinged with republicanism and were claimed by republican activists as protests against the monarchy of Louis Philippe. For the young Marx, the Lyon weavers were 'the soldiers of socialism' (Marx, 1975 [1844], p. 418). But for others, they appear proud, skilled workers driven to desperation by economic change that was out of their control.

Unpicking experiences

EXERCISE

In the preceding sections I have discussed a wide range of different kinds of industrial workers – the kinds of individuals that we might label as producers.

1   Note down the various work environments that are either implicit or explicit in what you have just read; note also how these environments appear to have been changing.

Table 18.1   Percentage of working population employed in agriculture from the earliest available censuses

Country	Date	Percentage
Austria	1869	68
Belgium	1846	51
Denmark	1850	60
Finland	1754	82
France	1856	54
Germany	1882	47
Great Britain	1841	26
Hungary	1857	74
Ireland	1841	53
Italy	1871	64
The Netherlands	1849	53
Norway	1891	57
Poland	1897	70
Portugal	1890	65
Spain	1860	72
Sweden	1860	67
Switzerland	1880	42
Russia	1926	82

(Source: Bairoch, 1975, p. 468)

2   I have concentrated on the industrial worker, what other sort of worker do you think was significant in the early nineteenth century? Table 18.1 should make the answer obvious. Does anything strike you as significant about the information in this table?

3   Was there anything specific about the workers' diets?

4   What element other than economics appears to have been involved in the disorders described?

Spend about 15 minutes on this exercise.

SPECIMEN ANSWER

1   Weavers (of cotton, linen and silk – generally working at home); some factory workers in textile production (all those mentioned here have actually been English); iron workers (whose industry boomed at the end of the eighteenth and beginning of the nineteenth centuries); miners. The Silesian weavers were threatened by mechanisation in both cotton and linen production; some Luddites felt threatened by the factory and some also by cheap female labour; the Lyon weavers felt threatened by cheap rural labour. In many of the instances described so far, the protests also arose because of attempts to impose reduced pay or new practices.

2   No specific mention has been made so far of work in agriculture. In fact, over much of continental Europe, agricultural workers continued to dominate the labour force up until the First World War, and in some states even beyond. This is a point that is often forgotten as a result of the focus on the process of industrialisation in nineteenth-century Europe.

3   Potatoes were a staple for the Silesian workers and bread was a staple for English workers; poor crops and bad harvests meant widespread distress.

4   In several of the disorders there were links with political agitation and excitement. Also, Wolff described the Silesian weavers singing a poem to a popular melody that was 'the Marseillaise of the needy'. There doesn't appear to have been anything overtly political about the weavers, but Wolff is trying to give them a slant in that direction (rather like the desire by French republicans to claim the Lyon silk weavers).

I want now to look at each one of these issues separately.

Work environments

The concept of industrialisation can involve two distinct analytical definitions. In the first of these, it defines a major shift in the distribution of the labour force from the agricultural (the primary) sector to the manufacturing (the secondary) sector of an economy. In the second, it defines a significant increase in technological innovation involving the substitution of inanimate power for human and animal effort, and the displacement of many manual skills by machine operations.

Britain in the eighteenth and early nineteenth centuries was the first to experience a major industrialisation process. (Compare, for example, the percentage of its labour force working in agriculture and the date given in Table 18.1.) This process was driven largely by textile production. Initially, this mainly involved cotton. There was a succession of technological inventions and innovations, each generally devised to break a bottleneck in the production process created by its predecessor. But the process was never entirely linear in the sense of a steady, uninterrupted growth of factory labour at the expense of everything else. Cotton industrialisation in the late eighteenth century, for example, led to an enormous growth in handloom weavers who worked at home. Within a couple of generations, however, the industrialisation process also led to their destruction, as new machines were introduced that replaced them. The basic work in the new cotton factories was unskilled labour generally undertaken by women and children. While it is common to think of the new work environment as harsh and immiserating, there were workers who could do well. The men who built and maintained the machines are a good example, and such men were often responsible for the technological innovations and inventions that drove the process forward.

Increased production requires an increase in raw materials and an increased market. The British merchant marine was large and efficient and could bring raw cotton easily from the Americas. Moreover, naval success in the wars against revolutionary and Napoleonic France, and the destruction of French colonies and overseas trade, opened up the world to British manufacturers seeking raw materials and new markets for their new, mass-produced goods. Victory in the wars with Napoleon opened hitherto protected European markets to these goods – to the detriment of, for example, Silesia.

Not all raw materials came from overseas. Each country is unique in its available natural resources. Britain was especially fortunate with the availability of water to power the early machines in factories that could be built not too far from ports where raw cotton could be landed. She also had coal and iron fields close to each other and of the quality that was needed for the kind of production that was wanted. War gave a boost to iron production, and, correspondingly, peace brought problems. After Waterloo, the entrepreneurs who had invested heavily in coal and iron sought new markets; iron docks and iron churches were built.

The appearance and spread of railways from the 1830s gave a new, and much needed, boost to the production of iron and steel across Europe. Small producers went under as iron and steel production, of necessity, became concentrated in major plants. The construction of railways required a tough, mobile workforce to build them. Large gangs of navvies who, in Britain, had originally dug canals (hence the name 'navvy' from 'navigators'), cut the lines and laid the tracks. They also commonly generated panic, sometimes justifiably, as a result of their rowdy behaviour. The burgeoning cities and towns required smaller gangs of builders who relied on quarries and brick makers to supply their materials.

Different industries grew up in and developed different environments. Initially, factories were in relatively rural environments where there was sufficient fast-flowing water to power machines. The industrial town centred on coal-fired factories emerged in a second wave of industrial development; but such towns grew rapidly. Miners were important to such developments, but miners lived close by their pits and consequently, as well as being key industrial workers, they were often rural dwellers in relatively small, closed communities.

The focus on industrialisation and the growth of industrial towns and cities can easily obscure the continuing importance and size of the agricultural sector of the early nineteenth-century economy. The people in fast-growing urban centres had to be fed. Indeed, it is accepted that, without massive improvements in agriculture that released money for investment and enabled a large urban-based manufacturing workforce to exist, then there could have been no industrialisation. While there was little mechanisation in farming in the first two-thirds of the nineteenth century, across the continent there was a similar pattern of developments: holdings were enlarged and consolidated; wastelands were drained; new and improved breeds of cattle and sheep were introduced to the land. At the same time, there were significant developments in land tenure and labour. Agricultural workers in Britain had not been bound to the land and lords for generations. Common land had begun to be enclosed in Tudor times, restricting the labourer's ability to keep an animal and some fowls. Enclosure and restrictions on the right to glean from recently harvested fields or to pick up fallen wood from forests for fuel gathered pace from the eighteenth century. The situation was similar on continental Europe, except here it also went hand in hand with the emancipation of the peasantry (see Table 18.2). It is important to appreciate, however, that the experience of change was different in different regions. Moreover, the process of change followed different timescales and contrasting patterns across different countries and regions – remember, for example, the contrast between *barshchina* and *obrok* in tsarist Russia that was discussed in Unit 16.

Table 18.2   Initial decrees of peasant emancipation

Country	Date
Savoy	1771
Baden	1783
Denmark	1788
France	1789
Switzerland	1798
Prussia	1807
Bavaria	1808
Württemberg	1817
Saxony	1832
Austria	1848
(Another 10 German states)	1848–1849
Hungary	1853
Russia	1861

(Source: Blum, 1978, p. 356)

Note that the dates given in Table 18.2 are for the 'initial' decrees of emancipation; the process was often not completed for many years and required additional legislation. In southern Italy, for example, feudalism was abolished by the Napoleonic regime but squabbles over land and land rights continued throughout the nineteenth century: notably, for example, during the revolutions of 1848 (see Anthology Document 5.19a). As you can see, a cluster of abolition occurred in the German lands during this wave of revolution (see Anthology Document 5.19b). Peasants bound under the vestiges of feudalism were occasionally seen as having an easy life (see Anthology Documents 5.19c and d). Equally, they could be exploited, far more than the law allowed, to force more labour or produce out of them, by landowners who circumvented or simply ignored the legal requirements. At times, landlords or their agents were murdered. Occasionally there were savage peasant uprisings, such as that which swept through the Austrian province of Galicia in 1846. The authorities in many states looked nervously at their peasantry and tried to decipher what they could of peasant opinion (see Anthology Document 5.19e). It can easily be assumed that emancipation was a good thing for the peasantry. For some there was the opportunity to acquire land and to create a significant holding. But emancipation often also meant providing some form of compensation to the old feudal landlord; in Prussia, for example, the peasantry was required to hand over about a third of the country's land to the gentry in compensation. And if a few peasants did well, emancipation meant that many more were pushed into becoming landless labourers who wandered the roads looking for work or alms, or who gravitated towards the cities. Moreover, the pattern of land tenure varied from country to country and from region to region.

Just as land tenure varied, so no two routes to an industrialised society were the same. Each region had its own advantages and problems of natural resources. Britain was fortunate in having good inland waterways for transport, which were easily enhanced by canals, and good overseas links. Raw materials in the shape of coal and iron ore were easily available and, equally important for production, in close proximity to each other. France was less fortunate in its availability of coal and iron. Its agricultural and financial structures also fostered a pattern of industrialisation different from that in Britain. There were major cotton factories in the sprawling urban conurbation that grew up around Lille in northern France in the early nineteenth century, but overall the country and the workforce remained much more rural (compare the percentage of agricultural workers in Britain and France given in Table 18.1). French entrepreneurs continued to rely on out-working for much production, and peasant families, often living on their own small properties thanks to the pattern of land ownership that emerged from the revolutionary upheavals and Napoleonic Code, were readily available for this. Remember the clause in the Civil Code that required the equal division of inheritance (Unit 17, p. 14 and Anthology Document 5.3). There were ways for individuals to get round this law and to give a lion's share to the eldest son, but it ensured that nineteenth-century France remained a country with thousands of small landowners.

EXERCISE

Read Anthology Document 5.12, 'Memoirs of a young journeyman', and note down what is being described here and what kind of workers are involved.

Spend about 5 minutes on this exercise.

SPECIMEN ANSWER

It is a description of joining a workers' association and then setting off on a countrywide tour. The workers involved are skilled craftsmen – joiners. They have contacts across the country who organise work when individuals arrive in a town or region. The association has strict rules of hierarchy and community; its members are proud of their association and fight with members of other bodies.

There remained large numbers of skilled craftsmen in nineteenth-century Europe. The 'tour of France' was just one route for young artisans as they sought to perfect their skills and planned to move up the ladder from journeyman to master. In Germany, such a tour was known as *das Wanderjahre*, in England it was simply 'going on the tramp'. The tour enabled a man to learn variations in technique and to work under a variety of mentors in what were, generally, small workshops. Associations such as the French *compagnonnage* could act like trade unions in some instances, negotiating with masters over wage rates and conditions and acting against masters who treated the *compagnons* badly. In general, the practice of the tour appears to have declined from the 1840s (see Figures 18.2 and 18.3).

Standards of living

There have been heated arguments between academics about the impact of the industrialisation process on the living standards of the people involved in that process. 'Pessimists', drawing initially on the bleak assessments of parliamentary enquiries and the accounts of early social investigators, have painted a grim picture of dark, unhealthy working-class slums in grimy, smoke-filled industrial towns, and of long hours and sometimes dangerous work in factories and mines. 'Optimists' have responded with wage and cost-of-living statistics and have pointed to the fact that much of the product of textile industrialisation was consumed by home markets and that factory labour offered more regular employment and proper wages rather than seasonal labour and payment in kind. 'Pessimists' responded with their statistics of mortality rates, unemployment, and food and drink consumption. In Germany in the 1830s and 1840s, for example, a large number of unskilled urban workers appear to have been getting a major percentage of their energy from their high consumption of *Branntwein* or *Schnaps* (only fats produce more energy more efficiently). This, in turn, led to a boom in the production of alcohol from potatoes, rather than from grain; and production shifted from the home or the small-scale workshop to the factory.

The people who produced were, of course, also consumers. But there is a series of problems with assessing standard-of-living issues. First, there is the problem of evidence. As you can see from the preceding paragraph, literary evidence has been contrasted with statistical evidence, and then one set of

Figure 18.2 A worker on the tour of France sets off from one town to another. He is followed by his fellow *compagnons*. They pretend to try to restrain him before bidding him farewell and wishing him a safe journey. From *L'Illustration*, 22 November 1845. Photo: Roget Viollet / Rex Features Ltd

Compagnons du tour de France. — Arrivée chez la mère.

Figure 18.3 A *compagnon* arrives at the next stop on his tour. Here he is greeted by the 'mother', who is the proprietor of a local *cabaret* that acts as the local base for his brotherhood. She introduces him to the 'roller', seated at the table and ready to find him employment in the district. From *Journées illustrées de la Révolution de 1848*, Paris 1848-49, p.95. Photo: The British Library

statistics has been set against another, different, set. Sometimes the statistics, such as mortality rates, were collected at the time; sometimes, as in the case of cost-of-living indices, they have been constructed from surviving wage rates and surviving records of rents, food and fuel prices. Some topics have only been studied regionally, which can create difficulties for an overall assessment of a single country, let alone for Europe as a whole. Regional differences, for example, could be the result of preference, availability, transport costs and a variety of other variables. Overall, it seems probably fair to say that many skilled workers, especially metalworkers and engineers, saw an improvement in their living standards while unskilled workers, both urban and rural, suffered real hardship for much of the early nineteenth century.

As consumers, all sections of the working class needed their daily bread to be able to work. Bread (or sometimes potatoes, or even, in parts of Italy for example, rice) was often the staple of a working family's diet. Meat and dairy produce were rarely consumed except on special occasions; in some regions, fruit and vegetables were equally rare in the diet of the poor. Food, and particularly bread, absorbed a high percentage – anything from 60 to 80 per cent in a reasonable year – of the family income. The consequence was that, in pre-industrial economies and in the industrialising economies of the late eighteenth and early nineteenth centuries, the harvest and the cost of food had great significance.

EXERCISE

Anthology Document 5.13, 'Food riots', comprises letters and reports about different incidents of food rioting in the late eighteenth and early nineteenth centuries. Read these now and answer the following questions.

1 What could be the cause of food shortages?

2 What different attitudes do you find among the correspondents in these letters?

3 What different forms could the food riots take?

Spend about 20 minutes on this exercise.

EXERCISE

1 Laîné (Anthology Document 5.13c) mentions the effects of the weather on the French harvest of 1816. In this instance it was rain, then snow, at the time of harvest. But problems might also arise from too much rain or a lack of it much earlier in the growing season. There were also threats from bugs and diseases. The terrible Irish famine of 1846 was the result of a disease (*Phythophthora infestans*) that destroyed the potato crop.

2 The Reverend Haden (Anthology Document 5.13b) appears to have a relatively sympathetic attitude to the plight of the poor. He is concerned that some farmers might be withholding corn from the poor and, by implication, looking for the best possible price they can get. He is also concerned about deploying local volunteers to deal with rioters, fearing that, since their families were also suffering from the shortages, they might prove unreliable [remember this is the time of the revolutionary and Napoleonic wars – look back to the section called 'The bonny bunch of roses' in Unit 17]. We do not have to look too closely at his letter to see that he is taking a rather different line to the trouble from the duke of Portland. The vicomte de Laîné, arguably, has a line similar to that suggested of Portland. He recognises the problems in his report, but writes in terms only of

rioters and mobs. The implication is, perhaps, that the poor should let the government deal with the problem by buying grain abroad as well as in the home market. It can be argued from this that government ministers were seeing a national problem of law and order while some men on the ground were witness to the immediate, day-to-day difficulties of the poor around them.

3 The important point is that food riots do not appear to have been mindless disorders. Laîné might write simply of mobs, but it is interesting to note that often they are attempting to prevent grain from being moved out of their district. There is rationality here. Perhaps a district did have a good harvest in comparison with others, but this would not prevent a fear that farmers in that district would move their harvest to where they could get the best prices. It is also interesting to note that in Cornwall the rioting tinners are described as paying for the corn that they have seized.

Social historians have shown considerable interest in the activities and mentalities of crowds, particularly those involved in food riots. In one of the most important analyses of this behaviour, Edward Thompson explored what he called the 'moral economy' of the eighteenth-century crowd (Thompson, 1991). Thompson saw 'legitimising notions' behind this crowd activity. Crowds had views of social norms and obligations, often rooted in Biblical verses. They considered that they had a right to food at a fair price and that it was morally outrageous for farmers, middle-men or millers to seek to profit at the expense of ordinary people. There were many among the crowd's social superiors who went along with such ideas. Such beliefs were not universal, but nor were they confined to England; a similar moral economy functioned in France, for example, where the name for crowd action in markets was *taxation populaire*.

Among the elites there appears to have been something of a change in the late eighteenth century as ideas of the importance of a free market took hold. In France, the attempt to enforce a free market during grain shortages towards the end of the eighteenth century worsened the situation during what became known as the 'flour war' (*la guerre des farines*). Magistrates in England who showed sympathy towards the moral economy, criticised profiteering farmers and middlemen, and sought to impose affordable prices in their localities were sharply rebuked by Portland and by subsequent home secretaries during food shortages in the first few decades of the nineteenth century. Portland and his successors were becoming wedded to free-market ideas. But there were important changes relating to production and consumption that helped to change first, the reliance of the workforce on a single staple, such as grain-made bread, and second, the disruptive linkage between high food prices and domestic industrial production.

When dominant industries depend on home demand, especially home demand from among the working class, then high prices tend to lead to a reduction in the demand for industrially produced goods. This, in turn, leads to a contraction in production with part-time working or lay-offs; the consequent reduction in pay serves to exacerbate the situation. This was a major problem

[handwritten margin notes:]

1783 – Prime Minister in Coalition

1807 – 1809 – PM

Sp. Percevol – Exchequer
Canning – F.O.
Castlereagh – War O.
Hawkesbury – Home Secretary
(Earl of Liverpool)

3rd Duke of Portland :–

William Henry Cavendish Bentinck

(1738 – 1809)

Home Secretary 1794 – 1801

P.H. Portland government

[inline handwritten notes:] natural leader of the Whigs. Married d. of 4th Duke of Devonshire,

(retired from office when Pitt died in 1806)

for British industry in the first half of the nineteenth century. The 1840s, christened 'the hungry forties', witnessed the worst example of this. Domestic consumption of cotton amounted to over 40 per cent of that produced in Britain; but overall, during this decade, domestic consumption contracted by about 50 percent. The situation improved, particularly after 1850, as exports absorbed a steadily increasing percentage of industrial output. At the same time, it became possible to bring in a wider variety of cheap food from both Europe and the Americas.

Politics and the workers

How far did the kinds of protest described above become involved with politics? I have noted that some Luddites had political aspirations and that political radicals at least appear to have sought to claim protesting workers as their own. I have also made reference to Chartists – but what was Chartism? And who were the Chartists?

EXERCISE

Anthology Document 5.14 is an extract from the first national petition of the Chartists to the British parliament. Read it now.

1   What is the petition demanding?

2   Why, according to the petition, are the Chartists making these demands?

3   What has been the problem with previous governments?

4   What is the justification for universal suffrage?

Spend about 5 minutes on this exercise.

SPECIMEN ANSWER

1   It wants parliament to introduce the People's Charter establishing its six points with reference to parliamentary elections and representation.

2   They want the reform because of what they see as the sorry state of the country – high taxes, starving and distressed workers, traders on the brink of bankruptcy, and all of this after nearly a quarter of a century of peace.

3   Previous governments have been full of factions only out for themselves.

4   Men are required to support and obey the laws, to defend the country (remember Cobbett, Anthology Document 5.10) and to pay taxes; they ought therefore to have a say in how laws are made and, effectively, in how the state is run.

Chartism was a genuinely working-class movement, but it was also uniquely British – there was nothing comparable on continental Europe. It can be seen as a movement continuing the old radical critique of corruption within government. But it was also significant in uniting working people on a specifically political platform that can be seen as the precursor of the oppositional politics that were to characterise the new industrial capitalist society. In some areas it involved middle-class radicals as well as people from the working class; though many of the former became alarmed and fell away at the fiery utterances of the so-called 'physical-force' Chartists, especially after the Newport rising (see above, pp. 43–4). Chartism drew on the recent experience of protest against the New Poor Law of 1834; to a great number of the working class, this appeared to stigmatise poverty and threaten the poor with imprisonment in the new workhouses, known as 'New Bastilles'. Chartism attracted factory workers, but among the leadership it was men with craft skills who dominated. An analysis of the 853 nominations to the National Charter Association's General Council in 1841 reveals the largest single group (130 men, or 15.2 per cent) to have been weavers, followed by shoemakers and cordwainers (14.8 per cent), tailors (6.8 per cent) and framework knitters (3.9 per cent) (Jones, 1975).

But if Chartism was a movement unique to the British Isles, political activism on the part of workers was not. As with the Chartists, the majority of the activists were men with craft skills rather than individuals whose work had been created by the new forces of industrialisation. But that, of course, is not to say that the trades of these activists were unaffected by new processes of the capitalisation of industry or new pressures generated by technological change and industrial organisation.

The involvement of artisans in politics across Europe in the first half of the nineteenth century was intermittent. A comparison of their behaviour in Britain, France and Germany has argued convincingly that, even in Chartism, they came together to resolve temporary injustices (Breuilly, 1992). They did not envisage politics as a continuing process of bargaining and debate between various interests. Nor did they seek to establish new institutional structures that would lead to a peaceful, democratic political environment. Artisan activity was much more often involved with their particular trade, with education, and with organising mutual assistance through co-operatives, benefit clubs and trade union activity. At the same time, there were a few artisans who were beginning to look beyond their own trade. In 1840, for example, a small group of Parisian artisans from a variety of trades established their own newspaper, *L'Atelier* (the workshop), which voiced hostility towards the growth of large-scale industry and changing work practices as well as towards the government. Like the Chartists, they considered that political reform was necessary to bring to power men who would put the people's interests first. Together with these artisans, there were radical activists who claimed to speak on behalf of, and sought to enlist the help of, workers. Such individuals commonly identified themselves as republicans or increasingly as socialists.

IDENTITY AND THE WORKPLACE

EXERCISE

Read Anthology Documents 5.15 'The prospectus for *L'Artisan, Journal de la Classe Ouvrière*, 1830', and 5.16 '*The Communist Manifesto*, 1848', and answer the following questions.

1   How would you characterise these two documents? They are not the same kind of document – what exactly are they?

2   What is the difference between the authors?

3   How far do these documents see workers as divided into separate trade groups?

4   Are there any similarities in the way that they describe workers?

5   Are there any similarities in the way that they describe other social groups?

Spend about 15 minutes on this exercise.

SPECIMEN ANSWER

1   Anthology Document 5.15 is the prospectus for a new newspaper written by and for members of the working class. Anthology Document 5.16 is an attempt to analyse society and to explain the direction in which it is moving; it is also a political manifesto prepared by members of an active, if fringe, radical group. While its tone and its analysis are polemical, it provides a stimulating survey of economic development over a long historical period – largely the period of this course.

2   The author(s) of the prospectus for *L'Artisan* are anonymous. They claim to be ordinary working printers and there is no reason to doubt their claim. The *Communist Manifesto*, in contrast, was written by educated young men keen to win people over to their political position and to their interpretation of economic and social development.

3   *L'Artisan* may be the work of print workers, but they claim to be speaking for all workers and see similar problems facing all workers. The *Communist Manifesto* sees the workers as divided among themselves and not recognising their true interests by fighting the bourgeoisie's old battles. Its authors believe, however, that the force of events will bring about union among proletarians and recognition of their strength and common needs.

4   In both documents, workers are described as a single social group facing similar pressures at the workplace. *L'Artisan* stresses the importance of what the worker does; the *Communist Manifesto* argues that pride and satisfaction is being driven from work by machines and exploitation.

5   In both cases, other social groups are regarded as, at best, unsympathetic to the plight of the workers. The *Communist Manifesto* argues that society is being increasingly divided into two groups – proletarians/working class and bourgeois/middle class. It recognises that, for the moment, there is a variety of social groups outside these two classes and that the working class is in conflict with some of them (remnants of the absolute monarchy, landowners, etc.), but ultimately it believes there will only be the two classes.

Class identity

You do not have to subscribe to Marxism to recognise that there was a growing awareness of the working class as a social group in the late eighteenth century and, especially, in the early nineteenth century. It is implicit in the two documents that you have just read; it is implicit in Chartism. In France, radical activists sought also to build on the tradition of Jacobinism from the French Revolution. And as Chartists argued that they had been let down by the Great Reform Act of 1832 by being denied the vote, so French working-class radicals argued that they had been let down by the outcome of the revolution of 1830. Workers, it was argued, had fought on the barricades and overthrown the restored Bourbon monarchy, but had not been rewarded by any recognition of their current economic plight, let alone any assistance. Essentially, however, the identity that emerged here for the working class was one defined by its economic position – it was a **working** class, *la classe **ouvrière**, die **Arbeiterklasse**.*

The class, according to the documents that you have just read, that was ranged against the working class was not labelled by its economic position however. It was the middle class or the bourgeois(ie) – *bourgeois* being the old French word for a town (*bourg*) dweller and usually someone with at least a little property. Just as the working class covered a range of trades, of labouring jobs and of economic stability, so the term middle class could embrace, at one end, very wealthy merchants, bankers and industrialists and, at the other, clerks on very meagre salaries.

Nevertheless, there is a difference between this 'class' identity and the way in which society was understood during the old regime. Under the old regime, society was divided into 'estates' or 'orders' of which there were three: nobility, clergy and everyone else. The division was not necessarily economic; there could be some poverty-stricken nobles and some extremely wealthy members of the third estate, and the clergy ran the gamut from prince-bishop to poor parish priest. The division was maintained by law and rested on privilege linked to social rank. In many old regime states, for example, which court it was that heard a criminal case against an individual could depend on that individual's estate; similarly, the kind of punishment that could be inflicted could depend on an individual's rank and privilege. There were significant variations across Europe, however. In England, for example, to all intents and purposes, there was equality before the law and Enlightenment thinkers commonly urged the adoption of such an English model of such equality. The French Revolution established equality before the law for France and held out the promise for elsewhere.

The Revolution (as noted in Unit 17) also employed the concept of the sovereignty of the people and the revolutionary and Napoleonic periods provided opportunities for such sovereignty to be exercised. Napoleon, however, did not wish to have a broad electorate voting for his assemblies, nor did the restored Bourbons for theirs. The electoral system established in early nineteenth-century France, and that established by the Great Reform Act in Britain in 1832, were progressive in the eyes of many in Europe in that they did not depend on the old privilege of birth, but they restricted the franchise to men with money and property. I have noted how members of the working class in Britain and France felt cheated by the way that events had turned out at the beginning of the 1830s. But they were not the only individuals who were deprived of the vote. I will return to the question of women later, but first it is worth remembering that there were other male individuals who were also deprived of the franchise or who felt that the old order still held too much sway. Moreover, in many parts of Europe, participation in the management of the state through the franchise was still denied to some of those defined by Marx and Engels as the bourgeoisie.

Class and revolution

The elites of restoration Europe feared a repetition of the French Revolution, and this anxiety became entangled with the growth of the new industrial society (remember Metternich's 'confession of faith', Anthology Document 5.9). I have already noted how, from different perspectives, different individuals interpreted events such as the uprisings in Lyon and Silesia. The anxieties were given substance by a series of revolutionary waves that swept across Europe in the early 1820s and, more significantly, in 1830 and 1848. Some of the early social enquirers investigating the living conditions of, particularly, the urban poor and trying to understand the causes of criminality were beginning to write of 'the dangerous classes'. The term was coined by a French police bureaucrat, Honoré Frégier, in a book published in 1840, *Des classes dangereuses de la population dans les des grandes villes et des moyens de les rendre meilleures* (*The Dangerous Classes of the Population in the Great Towns and the Means of Improving Them*). Marx, you will have seen, was beginning to develop ideas of class as being a key element in revolution. But how far was class identity central to these revolutionary outbreaks?

A variety of different social groups participated in the revolutions that swept through west and central Europe in 1848. Each group had its own agenda. Businessmen did not fight on the barricades, but many, probably most, had felt the impact of the economic difficulties of the 1840s. They were present in the revolutionary assemblies that were established during the revolutions; very occasionally, they were also present in the new ministries. Many were keen to reduce still further the authority of the vestiges of feudalism and aristocracy. But they also pressed policies designed to restore confidence and revive business and trade. Often the latter meant protectionism, something that was very strong among the business elite of France that argued for action to preserve *le travail national* (the work of the nation).

Students, together with some lawyers and doctors, were also active in the revolutions. Students fought alongside workers on barricades, though their grievances were very different. In Prussia and Vienna, in particular, the students were angered by what they considered to be an ossified professoriate and poor job prospects. Liberal and radical doctors and lawyers were united by what they considered to be a lack of economic and social status.

Peasants in central and eastern Europe resented the continuance of feudal obligation. Table 18.2 above notes the number of German states that took at least the first steps towards peasant emancipation under pressure of the upheaval of 1848. In France, where emancipation was completed during the 1790s and cemented by the Napoleonic codes, peasants used the opportunity of 1848 to try to take back common land and other 'rights'. They also refused to pay a new tax introduced by the provisional government established following the February Revolution. Some insisted that, since France had no king, no new taxes could be implemented. Elsewhere, peasants sometimes rallied to the monarch. The assumption was invariably that the 'good king' or 'good prince' was misled by corrupt, self-serving ministers, or pressurised by urban idlers. The ferocious peasant uprising in Galicia in 1846 (see above, p. 49) was directed against Polish gentry landowners who were sympathetic to Polish nationalism. The peasants claimed that they were acting against such traitors in defence of the Austrian emperor; though their hopes that the emperor would reward them by abolishing their labour commitments to the landowners were cruelly dashed. Similar sentiments were present in parts of central Europe in 1848. Nationalism was an ideology to be found among the gentry or among urban liberals and intellectuals; most peasants had little vision beyond their local community; they did not understand, let alone subscribe to, the concept of belonging to a 'nation'.

Workers, and especially artisans and journeymen, constituted the largest single group on the barricades in 1848. Sometimes their anger was directed towards master manufacturers and their behaviour was similar to that in Silesia in 1844. Sometimes they turned on foreign workers who they thought threatened their jobs; in France British textile-machine mechanics and Belgian canal workers were targets. They presented demands and petitions to improve their position at the workplace, to provide them with a greater say in the running of the state and to put them on a more equal standing with their social superiors. There was an Artisans' Congress in Frankfurt in July 1848. But perhaps the most significant worker activity, and initial worker success, during 1848 was to be found in France, especially in Paris.

EXERCISE

Read Anthology Document 5.17 'Decrees of the French national government, 25 February 1948'.

1   What sort of documents are these?

2   What are they establishing?

Spend about 5 minutes on this exercise.

SPECIMEN ANSWER

1   They are government decrees.

2   They are promising the right to work but also enacting a series of measures for the benefit of working people – the restoration of pawned goods (and the goods listed here, together with the value, gives an idea of the desperate plight of some workers); a hospital for people with industrial injuries; and a system of national workshops.

There is some debate about just what the provisional government intended by these decrees. The decrees were drafted with a crowd demonstrating in the street outside the building where the government was meeting; at one point, demonstrators broke into the room where the government was assembled. The national workshops meant much to the workers, many of whom envisaged them as a potential system for organising labour across the country. Most members of the government, however, appear to have considered them as something like the old system of charity workshops that provided relief for workers in distress. Louis Blanc urged the government to create a ministry of labour. The government refused and established the Luxembourg Commission, headed by Blanc and Albert, a token worker who had also joined the government. The commission was to investigate the problem of labour and present solutions for the new National Assembly that was to be elected for the restored republic. The question here too must be what did the government think it was doing with this commission? How far was it simply a means of shelving the problem of the workers for a while and getting Blanc and Albert out of the way? For the workers, in contrast, the commission was a significant commitment by the government and, given its recruitment from men elected by the Paris trades, it appeared to have potential for the way that the republic might be ordered in future.

EXERCISE

Read Anthology Document 5.18 '*Manifesto of the Delegates of the Corporations (at the Luxembourg) to the Workers ...*, 8 June 1848'.

1   Who are the authors and what is the audience they are addressing?

2   How do the authors understand the role of the producer?

3   In Unit 17 we discussed the concept of the sovereignty of the people. In what way is that 'sovereignty' deployed here?

Spend about 10 minutes on this exercise.

SPECIMEN ANSWER

1   The authors are workers (the delegates to the commission) and they are addressing fellow workers.

2   They understand the producer as central to the state and to society. Without the producer, the state could not function and the workers' social superiors could not enjoy any of the benefits that they have.

3   The document takes the notion of the sovereignty of the people and, equating the people with producers, is really suggesting that the producers (workers, proletarians) are the most important element within the state and within society. The state is the people, the people are producers, the people/producers are, therefore, ultimately sovereign.

But the workers had problems. France was still predominantly a rural country. While artisans and workers in other French towns and cities commonly shared the aspirations of their fellows in Paris, there was poor coordination between them. Tensions developed between the workers in Paris and the provisional government as it became clear to the former that the latter did not envisage the republic developing along the kind of lines envisaged by the workers. It also became clear that the government did not envisage developing the national workshops into a system for cooperatives run by workers' associations across the country. Indeed, on 21 June, the government issued a decree abolishing the workshops. The workers' response was a new insurrection (23–26 June) which was suppressed only by a massive military deployment (see Figures 18.4 and 18.5). About 1500 insurgents were killed and 11,600 arrested.

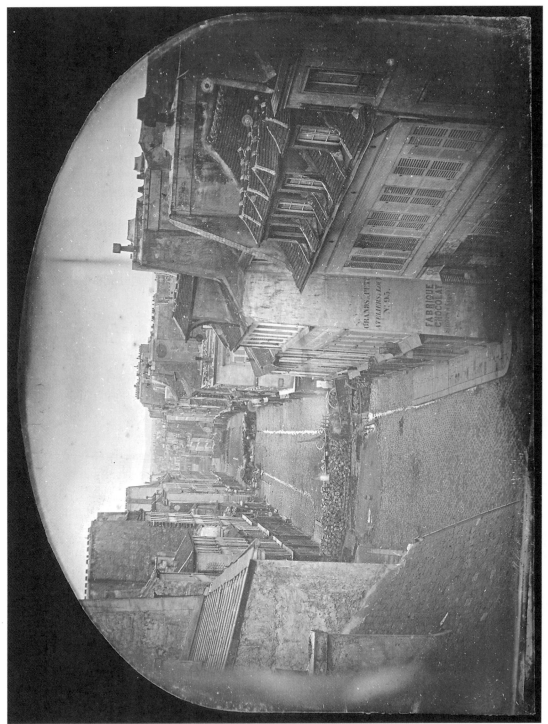

Figure 18.4 Thibault, Insurgents' Barricades in the rue Saint Maur, 25 June 1848, daguerreotype. Photo: © Sotheby's Picture Library. Rue Saint Maur is on the eastern side of Paris, north of the Seine: one of the principal workers' districts

Figure 18.5 Thibault , Barricades in Rue Saint-Maur after the attack of 25th June 1848, daguerreotype. Private Collection. Photo: Archives Charmet/ The Bridgeman Art Library. It shows French troops around the barricades after they had stormed and captured the road. The number of troops present in this one road gives an idea of the military deployment and the scale of the fighting

Class, childhood and gender

EXERCISE Look at Figures 18.6 and 18.7 and read Anthology Document 5.20 'Letter by Richard Oastler to the *Leeds Mercury*, 1830'.

1　What do the illustrations tell you about the factory workforce?

2　What does the document tell you about the factory workforce?

Spend about 10 minutes on this exercise.

Figure 18.6　Children working spinning machines in a textile mill in the 1820s, engraving. Photo: Getty Images

Drawn by T. Allom.

Engraved by J. Tingle.

Figure 18.7 Powerloom weaving, drawn by T. Allom, engraved by J. Tingle, from Edward Baines, *History of the Cotton Manufacture in Great Britain*, London: H. Fisher, R. Fisher & P. Jackson, 1835. Photo: Mary Evans Picture Library. Note how the machines are worked by leather belts driven by cylinders running across the ceiling

1   The workforce in the first illustration is made up of children – and from the look of the dresses they are all girls. A male worker, presumably a foreman, is inspecting some cloth in the second illustration but the workforce here is female. The illustrations give a rather romantic portrayal of the workers – they certainly look clean, healthy and well fed. This makes one wonder whether the figures (especially the children) were drawn from life and, if they were, whether this representation was typical of these early factories given other evidence.

2   The document is a furious attack on child labour in Yorkshire factories that draws a comparison between the wage slaves of Yorkshire (a county with strong support for the anti-slavery movement) and the chattel slaves of the colonies.

The employment of children was nothing new, nor was it restricted to the factory. In the pre-industrial world, children had worked in the fields as soon as they were old enough. If necessary, they worked as part of the family unit engaged in out-work, when a master entrusted the father with an order for the manufacture of cloth, for example, using looms and other equipment in the home. They worked in mines, sometimes going to the pits with their parents but taking on different tasks, such as pulling trucks of coal or ore underground, or, at the pit head, sorting what had been extracted. At an early age, girls were often sent into service and boys were often apprenticed. Apprenticeships were available in a variety of trades, some that could lead to a proper trade for the boy and some that could lead to an early grave. Alongside the concerns about factory labour, the early nineteenth century also witnessed a growing outcry about the 'apprenticeship' of climbing boys to master chimney sweeps.

What appears to have developed in the first half of the nineteenth century was an awareness of the concept of childhood. This was linked partly with a growth of sensibility and also with ideas of the innocence of children. The growth of the factory and the reports of small children forced to work long hours on the factory floor, often doing dangerous jobs – their size meant that they could be used to crawl into small spaces between unguarded machines to pick up waste or remove obstructions – probably intensified and gave a greater immediacy to these developments. Vigorous campaigns in several countries forced governments to take action with some initial, and limited, restrictions on the use of child labour from the early 1840s. Such legislation commonly applied only to the factory, and children still worked in the countryside, possibly beginning as crow scarers, or gleaning from the harvested fields alongside their mothers, until they were able to take on heavier and more physical tasks.

Now answer the following two questions, which are tangential to the topic of this section of the unit but very important for understanding the development of the nineteenth-century state.

1   What was the state doing with the factory legislation mentioned in the previous paragraph?

2   Have you come across states acting in such ways earlier in the course? Why is it interesting that the British state was among the first to develop such legislation?

Spend about 10 minutes on this exercise.

1 By this legislation, the state was seeking specifically to protect children from being required to undertake dangerous tasks by their employers. More generally, it shows the state becoming involved in the regulation of the workplace.

2 No. This really is a new departure for the bureaucratic state that emerged in nineteenth-century Europe. This kind of legislation heralds the beginning of what is usually described as the regulatory state, seeking to iron out and prevent abuses by use of the law and government inspectors. What is especially interesting in all of this is the fact that it was the British state – a state generally regarded as less centralised and less intrusive than most of those on continental Europe, that was in the forefront of this development.

Female labour, like child labour, was not something created by industrialisation. Unmarried women had worked for wages in pre-industrial societies. When families worked as a kind of labour unit at home, in mines or elsewhere, the labour of the wife was as central as, though often different from, that of the male family head. Separate spheres and male authority were as important within the peasant or artisan community as they were to the social and political elite. On a small farm, for example, any male peasant who did not appear the master could be the subject of ridicule by fellow villagers. In various forms of French, such unmanly behaviour was linked with chickens: he was a *tâte poule* (a chicken feeler in basic French), *tâtâ-dzeneille* (Swiss Canton of the Vaud), *tate mes glaines* (Picardy), *tâteux de poule* (Normandy), *coquefredouille* (Franche-Comté, where *coque* meant 'egg' and *fredouiller* meant 'feel') (Segalen, 1983, p. 115). And *la dispute de la culotte* (the quarrel over the breeches) was a motif found in several popular prints during the nineteenth century – see Figure 18.8. But industrialisation brought change to the traditional male/female, husband/wife, father/daughter relationship, particularly among the labouring population of the expanding urban areas.

The employment of larger numbers of women in factories was not popular with many male workers, especially when such men themselves were unemployed. The women were accused of 'taking' their jobs. It is difficult to assess changing levels of domestic violence. By definition, such violence takes place in the domestic sphere and, while people in crowded tenements might have heard it, and subsequently seen the cuts and bruises, often neither neighbours nor victims were prepared to take any action. One principal reason for this is that it was commonly accepted that, within reason, a man, as master of his family, had the right to chastise wife, servant and children for wrong-doing or for failure to complete tasks or duties. There is, however, some evidence of an increase in domestic violence on the part of some males in the early nineteenth century. Research in Germany has suggested that changing patterns of production that undermined the man's dominance in the household, combined with the economic crises of the 1840s and shifts in patterns of male sociability that increasingly focused on strong drink and the pub, fostered an increase in domestic violence. Women victims responded, in increasing

Civil Code of 1804, which meant hen were more equal than women.

Figure 18.8 *The Quarrel over the Breeches*, nineteenth century, engraving by Imprimerie Pellerin. Le Musée national des Arts et Traditions populaires, Paris. Photo: © RMN / © Jean-Gilles Berizzi. Showing an argument in a French peasant family over who 'wears the trousers'. The man holds a stick, the woman a distaff, her spinning wheel and the children's toys (drum and doll) are scattered across the floor

numbers, by going to civil law and seeking a divorce (Abrams, 1996). A similar picture has been painted for England in the same period, but here the possibility of divorce or legal separation was more remote. The response appears to have been an increasing use of folkloric shaming punishment directed by women themselves, or the use of the criminal justice system with a prosecution for assault; many victims, however, appear to have stopped short of the actual prosecution, hoping that the threat would be sufficient to stop any such beatings (Emsley, 2005, pp. 60–4). A study of murder in the department of the Nord, one of the regions of France most marked by industrialised production during the nineteenth century, has concluded that these changes affected the pattern of the offence. By the end of the century, when home-based production had been replaced by departure in the early morning for the factory, domestic murder was increasingly involving individuals in the big industrial cities and people from non-propertied groups (Parrella, 1992).

INDUSTRIAL SOCIETY AND NATIONAL SOCIETY

So far in this unit there has been some discussion of the growth of class identity linked with changing economic processes. It has been suggested that people began identifying with similar work groups beyond their native region and, sometimes, there was also an international dimension to this identification (at least in the minds of intellectuals such as Marx and Engels). In Paris, at least, some workers in 1848 were identifying themselves as the 'people' and as 'producers', and hence as the key element in the state. Some were prepared to fight and die for their 'class' and for what they understood as the legitimate demands of that class. In Unit 17 there was some discussion of the development of ideas of the nation and the nation state during and immediately after the period of the French Revolution and Napoleon.

EXERCISE

1   Do you think that ideas of class and of belonging to a nation were complementary or contradictory in this period?

2   Can you think of any way in which the process of industrial change might be linked with the way in which people came to adopt the idea of belonging to a nation?

Spend about 10 minutes on this exercise.

DISCUSSION

These are not easy questions; historians continue to debate them and there are no absolute answers, so I have not provided a specimen answer this time, just a discussion.

1   In the extracts from the *Communist Manifesto* that you read, Marx and Engels argue that 'national one-sidedness and narrow-mindedness' were becoming more and more impossible with the changes in production. Class divisions, they maintained, were becoming more acute and sweeping away others. In the unit I have mentioned both Galician peasants supporting the multi-ethnic Austrian empire and turning on their landowners, who saw themselves as Poles and wanted Polish independence, and French workers turning on Belgians and British in their country. Marx and Engels acknowledged such behaviour but

insisted that it would eventually disappear. Subsequently workers who put nation before class were labelled by Marxists and by other radicals (sometimes activists, sometimes academics) as blinded by a false consciousness manufactured particularly in the school and barracks. But then, what is the evidence for the assertion of false consciousness? Isn't this just a way to explain away facts that don't fit the theory?

2   In a series of books and articles, the eminent sociologist Ernest Gellner argued that modern nationalism came about largely through the kinds of changes in society that contributed to the industrialisation process. Agrarian societies, he argued, have little need to look far beyond the borders of their village or, at most, their local market. Individuals in small agrarian societies associated themselves with, and identified with, their village community. They might not speak the same language as their rulers, and this did not matter. The industrial process, in contrast, required a literate, mobile population and significant expansion in communications. Literate, mobile populations do not associate in small local communities and need a shared language to be able to communicate beyond such communities. The nation state, Gellner argued, emerged as a logical and effective way to manage modern, industrialised social entities.

In Gellner's words:

> The earlier society based on agricultural production and on a stable technology was more or less doomed to a military–clerical ethos, to hierarchy, dogmatism, cultural plurality, a tension between a high and low culture, and a political system based on power structures and religious ideology, but generally indifferent to cultural similarities. It proliferated differences related to social positions but not to political boundaries. The new society, based on expanding technology, semantic not physical work, on persuasive impersonal and often anonymous communication by means of context-free messages, and on an unstable occupational structure, is destined for a standardized, educationally transmitted high culture, more or less completely and persuasively diffused among its members. Its political or authority structures will be legitimated by two considerations – whether they can ensure sustained economic growth, and whether they can engender, diffuse and protect the culture which is the idiom of the society in question. Polity and high culture will thus become intimately linked, and the old links between polity and faith or dynasty will be dissolved, or reduced to a merely decorative, rather than genuinely functional, status. The state is the protector of a culture and not a faith.
>
> (Gellner, 1996, p. 110)

Does this mean then that nationalism was a creation of the nineteenth-century European state and its apologists? Well, that is an issue for the next unit.

REFERENCES

Abrams, L. (1996) 'Companionship and conflict: the negotiation of marriage relations in the nineteenth century' in Abrams, L. and Harvey, E. (eds) *Gender Relations in German History: Power, agency and experience from the sixteenth to the twentieth century*, London, UCL Press.

Bairoch, P. (1975) 'Agriculture and the Industrial Revolution 1700–1914' in Cipolla, C.M. (ed.) *The Fontana Economic History of Europe. The Industrial Revolution*, 2nd edn, London, Fontana–Collins.

Blum, J. (1978) *The End of the Old Order in Rural Europe*, Princeton, Princeton University Press.

Breuilly, J. (1992) 'Artisan economy, ideology and politics: the artisan contribution to the mid-nineteenth-century European labour movement' in *Labour and Liberalism in Nineteenth-Century Europe: Essays in Comparative History*, Manchester, Manchester University Press.

Emsley, C. (2005) *Hard Men: The English and Violence since 1750*, London, Hambledon.

Gellner, E. (1996) 'The coming of nationalism and its interpretation: the myths of nation and class' in Balakrishnan, G. (ed.) *Mapping the Nation*, London, Verso.

Jones, D.J.V. (1975) *Chartism and the Chartists*, London, Allen Lane.

Marx, K. (1975 [1844]) 'Critical notes on the article "The king of Prussia and social reform. By a Prussian"' in *Early Writings*, Harmondsworth, Penguin (first published in *Vorwärts!*, no. 64, 10 August 1844).

Parrella, A. (1992) 'Industrialization and murder: northern France 1815–1914', *Journal of Interdisciplinary History*, vol. 22, no. 4, pp. 627–54.

Segalen, M. (1983) *Love and Power in the Peasant Family: Rural France in the Nineteenth Century*, Oxford, Basil Blackwell.

Thompson, E.P. (1991) 'The moral economy of the English crowd in the eighteenth century' in *Customs in Common*, London, Merlin Press (first published in *Past and Present*, no. 50, 1971).

Paul Lawrence

INTRODUCTION

Without a country you have no name, no identity, no voice, no rights,
no membership in the brotherhood of nations – you remain just the
bastards of humanity. Soldiers without a flag, Jews in a world of
Gentiles, you will win neither trust nor protection. You will have no
sponsors. Do not be misled into trying to achieve your emancipation
from an unfair social condition until you have freed your country. You
will not succeed in such an effort. Only your country, the blessed land
that stretches spacious and rich between the Alps and the southern rim
of Sicily, can realize your hopes of a better lot.

(Giuseppe Mazzini, quoted in Silone, 1937, p.30)

During the course of the nineteenth century, quite a number of new countries
came into being. The Greece we know today, for example, dates only from
1830, Belgium from 1830–1, Italy from 1861 and Germany from as late as
1871. The nineteenth century also witnessed the decline of multinational states
such as the Ottoman empire, and the consolidation of national identity in
existing countries such as England and France. This unit (and also Unit 20)
will investigate these processes a bit further. How, and why, did these
important changes occur? As we have seen in the previous units of this block,
the period between about 1750 and around 1850 was one in which significant
new ideas about the role of the state and its relationship to 'the people' arose.
In the wake of the French Revolution, it appears that changes took place in the
way in which governments were expected to relate to those under their charge.
Towards the end of the eighteenth century, most people lived in countries
where they were considered 'subjects', under the command of royalty and a
hereditary aristocracy. By the mid nineteenth century, however, and certainly
by the start of the twentieth century, many (if not most) people in Europe saw
themselves as 'citizens' of 'nation states'.

As noted in Unit 17, the French Revolution has often been described (not least
by those involved at the time) as the crucible in which both the modern nation
and a modern sense of national sentiment were first forged, before being
disseminated more widely. Certainly, there is some evidence to support this
viewpoint. After all, the *Declaration of the Rights of Man and the Citizen*
proclaimed by the revolutionaries in August 1789 specifically claimed that 'the
principle of all sovereignty lies fundamentally with the nation; no body, no
individual can exercise authority which does not expressly emanate from it'
(Baycroft, 1998, p. 10). In addition to the spread of new ways of thinking
about government, a brief glance at the nineteenth century shows that there
were a lot of new countries at the end of it which did not previously exist.
After a war with Austria and a number of internal struggles, Italy, for example,

was finally unified in 1861. These events caused great excitement in Europe, and the British prime minister, Gladstone, called Italy 'the most stupendous fabric that had ever been erected on the basis of human integrity in any age or country of the world' (quoted in Fulbrook, 1993, p. 46). Quotations such as this again seem to support the view that the nineteenth century saw the dawning of an 'age of nationalism' when European peoples awoke to self-awareness, decided they wanted to govern their own affairs and shrugged off the last vestiges of feudal privilege. However, this unit will ask whether this view is really as unproblematic as it might at first seem.

Unfortunately for us, as you will see, this neat picture is a little too simplistic, and does not always fit the facts. To take the example of Italy once more, there are significant doubts about the extent to which national or patriotic sentiment was felt by the bulk of the population in 1861. In fact, one of the prime movers in the process of unification, Massimo d'Azeglio, is believed to have said in 1861 'We have made Italy, now we have to make Italians'. Moreover, unification was actually far from complete in 1861. Rome and the Veneto were under the sovereignty of foreign powers, and much of southern Italy was in a state of open civil war. As such, any simplistic depiction of patriotic Italians throwing off the yoke of the oppressor and realising their common heritage begins to look rather shaky. Even in more established countries the picture is by no means simple. Countries such as England and France had existed in more or less their current form for hundreds of years by the end of the nineteenth century. Surely here, then, national identity and a sense of patriotic belonging would be fairly easy to detect? Actually, when one starts to consider historical evidence, rather than simply the claims of nationalists, a somewhat less certain picture develops. The exercise below will help to illustrate this point.

EXERCISE

I would like you to read and compare two primary source extracts, both of which have something to say about national identity in France. Anthology Document 5.21, 'Ernest Renan's *Qu'est-ce qu'une nation? (What is a nation?)*', (of which I would like you to read just parts 1, 3 and 4 for now) is from a famous lecture on nationalism by the nineteenth-century French theologian Ernest Renan. Anthology Document 5.22, 'French ministerial circular, 14 August 1925', is a governmental circular concerned with the use (or lack of it) of the French language in different regions of France. As you read the documents, think about the following question – what do these documents indicate to you about nature and strength of French national identity? There is no need to write out an answer in full, but you may wish to underline any words or phrases that seem particularly striking in the excerpts, and to jot down a few notes summarising them.

Spend about 30 minutes on this exercise.

SPECIMEN ANSWER

It is apparent, if rather confusing, that two very different views of national identity are presented here. Renan's rather romantic view of a nation as a 'soul' and as a 'spiritual principle' claims that national sentiment is something that occurs naturally, and that rests on a long-shared history which gradually draws together all members of a nation. He claims, moreover, that France was the first modern nation, and others merely imitate France's glory. Clearly, Renan has no doubts as to the unity of France and the full participation of all in the national project. The second extract, by contrast, appears to show that, even in 1925, members of the French government were worried about the extent of national unity. In many regions of France, dialects (or *patois*) very different to Parisian French were still being spoken. This would appear to indicate a certain fragility of identity – with regional cultures perhaps competing with the national, French, culture. Far from Renan's 'rich legacy of remembrances' and 'common will in the present', the second extract appears to indicate that an active governmental hand is necessary to ensure that French identity remains viable. It is striking that Renan's claims that linguistic unity has never been forced in France seem somewhat dubious in the light of the second extract.

This exercise illustrates one of the things we have to get used to when studying the rise of nation states and growth of national identity – the fact that these are very complex phenomena, and hence they often throw up rather contradictory and subjective evidence. Continuing with the example of France, how is it that Baron Haussmann, the architect of much of modern Paris, could refer in his memoirs to 'our country, the most "one" in the whole world' (quoted in Weber, 1977, p. 9) while (writing scarcely a decade before) Léon Gambetta, one of the founders of the French Third Republic, believed that there was, intellectually speaking, 'an enormous distance' between outlying regions of France and 'the enlightened part of the country', and a vast gulf between 'those who speak our language and those many of our compatriots [who], cruel as it is to say so, can no more than stammer in it' (quoted in Weber, 1977, p. 10). Which view of France is the 'correct' one? Both men believed what they were writing and both paint a compelling portrait of France. Hence, there are no easy answers when thinking about nations and nationalism, which can often mean different things to different people. If we consider contemporary British society, for example, it is readily apparent that we often possess multiple identities which overlap. It is perfectly possible to define oneself as both Muslim and British, both a Yorkshireman and English, both a Christian and a Scot. Which identity comes to the fore depends very much on context. Moreover, even when national identity (as opposed to religious or regional identity) is considered, this is not a single, coherent entity. If you ask twenty people what being British means to them, you are very likely to get twenty different answers.

For this reason, before we go on to explore the subject further, I would like briefly to outline some of the terminology you will encounter in this unit. Precisely because some of the issues we will cover can be quite complex, it is important to be clear and precise in our use of language. Take your time reading these next paragraphs, and do reread them if necessary. Generally speaking, the term '**state**' will be used below to refer to the apparatus of government pertaining to a particular geographical area. Thus, a 'state' is primarily an administrative and political entity. By contrast, the term '**nation**' is much harder to define. Essentially, however, a 'nation' will be defined more in terms of cultural attributes. A nation, then, is a named human population, usually sharing a given territory, usually having a shared cultural history, often (but not always) speaking the same language and normally conscious of the fact that they constitute a nation. This last point is crucial. As Ernest Gellner (1983) has noted, two men (or women) are of the same nation if they share the same culture (where culture is sociologically defined as a system of ideas and signs and associations and ways of behaving and communicating), but also only if they *recognise* each other as belonging to the same nation. The sense of belonging to a distinct cultural nation is usually called 'national identity'.

As you may have noticed from these definitions, nations and states have not always overlapped. Large empires (or 'states') such as the Habsburg and Ottoman empires at one time contained many different distinct 'nations'. Equally, some modern 'nations' (such as Germany) were in the past subdivided into numerous smaller governing principalities (or 'states'). During the course of the nineteenth century, however, it came to be seen as more and more desirable that each cultural nation should have a state of its own – in other words, that each identifiable nation should govern itself. Nations came to demand their own states – usually either by (violent) unification, as in Italy and Germany, or by succession, as in Greece. These new countries are normally referred to as **'nation states'** (i.e. one nation equals one state) and the idea that every nation should govern itself is usually referred to as the **'nation-state principle'**.

Before you despair of this unit, take heart – all will become clear and nothing more complicated than this lurks ahead. There is no disguising the fact, however, that the rise of 'nation states' and 'national identities' is a complex, slippery subject requiring precise terminology. To make matters worse, as we will see, historians have disagreed endlessly over the process. That said, it is worth bearing in mind that we are considering one of the most fundamental processes in the formation of the Europe in which we live in today. The historical developments explored in this unit and the next have had a great impact, not just on the way in which European societies are organised, but also on the way in which we think about ourselves and our fellow citizens. Given this, it is certainly worth spending a bit of time on it.

You will see that this unit is divided into three sections. The first, 'Nations – old and new', will give an overview of the rise of nation states in Europe during the nineteenth century. Broadly speaking, this first section will consider what actually happened – how and when new nation states came into being and the changes that happened in existing countries. However, it is, of course, important for historians not simply to *describe* historical change, but to attempt to explain it. Hence, this unit will also consider some of the major explanations put forward as to *why* this set of changes happened at this particular time. The second section of the unit 'The "modernity" of nation states' will highlight and illustrate some of the major explanations put forward by historians for the rise of nation states. Many historians believe that nation states are primarily modern phenomena and are intrinsically linked to the rise of modern, industrial society. However, as historians are an argumentative lot and do not always agree with each other (even when assessing the same evidence), the third section of the unit, '"When" is a nation?', will consider some counter-claims on the part of historians who believe that national identity is, in fact, much older than we might expect.

NATIONS – OLD AND NEW

This section of the unit aims to give you an overview of some of the major political, social and economic changes associated with the rise of nation states in Europe during the nineteenth century. The pace of social change, partly driven by industrialisation and rapid urbanisation in some countries, was really quite rapid during the nineteenth century, as the following introductory exercise will illustrate.

EXERCISE

I would like you to compare two maps of Europe (Figures 19.1 and 19.2) – one drawn up in 1815 after the Congress of Vienna (which you have already encountered in Unit 17) and one that depicts Europe a century later on the eve of the First World War. I would like you simply to note as many differences between the two maps as possible. In particular, which countries seem to have appeared, and which have changed in shape and/or size? Other than this list, there is no need to write down a formal answer for this exercise, but, as you work, think about the use of maps as historical sources and jot down some of their advantages and drawbacks for historical study. Also think about what questions historians might want to ask about specific maps and why.

Spend about 20 minutes on this exercise.

SPECIMEN ANSWER

There are a number of significant boundary changes that occurred between 1815 and 1914:

- the appearance of Greece, Bulgaria, Macedonia, Montenegro and Albania (all of which were previously part of the Ottoman empire) as distinct countries in their own right

- the appearance of Romania, also previously part of the Ottoman empire

- the unification of Italy from a number of smaller states, some of which had been under the control of the Austrian empire

- the amalgamation of a number of German-speaking states into the German empire

- the appearance of Belgium following its succession from the Netherlands.

[handwritten annotation: secession]

Maps are obviously, in some ways, extremely helpful resources for the historian. However, they do need to be used with caution. A map should always be treated in the same way as any other historical source – with a healthy degree of scepticism. Maps are vital historical evidence but must be interpreted cautiously and carefully. They should not be used in isolation. Related documents may give information about accuracy, purpose, method of production and uniqueness, or may confirm map details. Such documents may be essential for full use of the map. Questions a historian might want to answer before trusting a map would include:

- When was the map made? The date of map information relates to the date the information was collected, not necessarily the publication date.

- What is the publication history of the map? Is this the earliest version of the map, or has the information been copied or compiled from previous maps?

- Why was the map made and for whom was the map intended? No map can show all available information. Mapmakers select information to suit the purpose of the map.

- What bias might the mapmaker have? Has the map been prepared to make a political point? Maps can make a powerful statement (for example, to show imperialist intentions or to establish nationhood).

DISCUSSION

A final potential drawback of maps for the historian, I believe, is that they can easily distance him or her from the object of study. Think about how easy it was simply to list the differences between the two maps. However, this very ease can perhaps lead us away from thinking about just how significant these changes were. Imagine what this complete redrawing of the map of Europe meant in human terms. Think of the turmoil, the bloodshed, the hopes and fears that such large-scale change inevitably entailed. While maps are an extremely useful tool to the historian, we must always be careful to retain a focus on the real object of our study – lives past and the factors that help illuminate them.

Given the vast social changes implied by the redrawing of the map of Europe outlined above, there is not space in a unit such as this to investigate all these developments equally. However, while the circumstances of national development varied extensively across Europe, three main processes can perhaps be identified – processes of unification (the amalgamation of existing smaller states), processes of succession (where new nation states were formed by breaking away from existing larger states) and processes of consolidation (whereby existing nation states became increasingly culturally homogenous, primarily through the erosion of regional identities). Why did these changes take place, however? Are there any broad factors that can be identified as contributing to these processes and can any similarities be detected between events in different parts of Europe? Let us look briefly at the formation of Italy and at Germany, as examples of processes of unification.

The situations of the territories that were to become Italy and Germany were not dissimilar after the Congress of Vienna at the start of the nineteenth century. In the eighteenth century, Germany had consisted of some 300 states, many of them tiny, all of them, including Prussia, still technically part of the Holy Roman Empire presided over by the Habsburg dynasty. The empire was abolished in 1806 and *der Deutsche Bund* (the German confederation), established in 1815, consisted of thirty-nine states, including Austria as well as Prussia. The confederation was the only all-German institution but it was a loose arrangement under permanent Austrian chairmanship and Prince Metternich was able to use the Diet at Frankfurt (an advisory assembly where the representatives of the states met), to thwart national and liberal aspirations. Italy, after the Vienna Settlement, consisted of ten political units: two

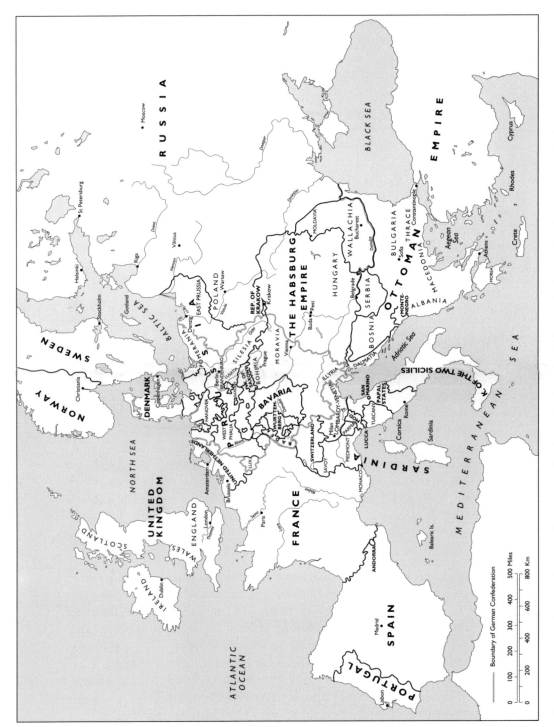

Figure 19.1 Map of Europe in 1815, from T.C.W. Blanning, ed., *The Oxford Illustrated History of Modern Europe*, Oxford: OUP, 1996, p.336-7. By Permission of Oxford University Press

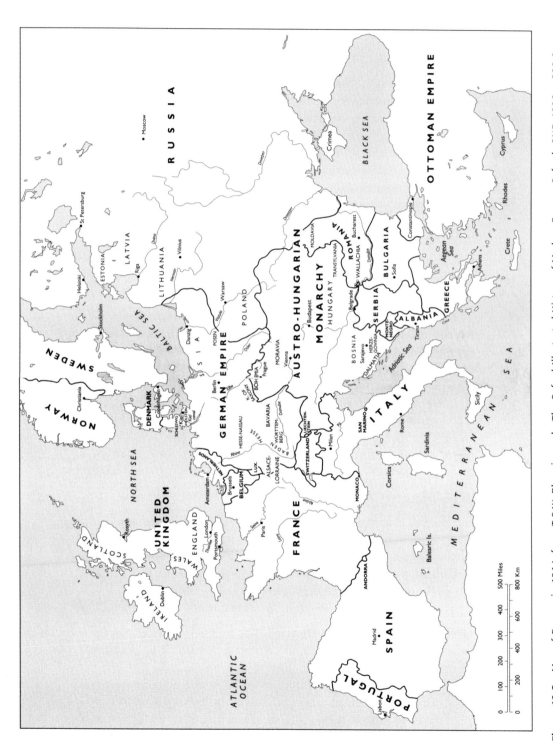

Figure 19.2 Map of Europe in 1914, from T.C.W. Blanning, ed., *The Oxford Illustrated History of Modern Europe*, Oxford: OUP, 1996, p.338-9.
By Permission of Oxford University Press

kingdoms, Sardinia (Sardinia and Piedmont) and the Two Sicilies (Sicily and Naples); the duchies of Parma, Modena, Massa and Carrara and, until 1847, the duchy of Lucca and the rather more important grand duchy of Tuscany; the Papal States; and Lombardy and Venetia, which were part of the Austrian empire. How did it happen that, from this diversity of states, two important nation states came into being?

One of the first factors that historians have often identified is an increase, during the latter part of the eighteenth century in particular, in philosophical and political treatises, poetry and cultural production generally celebrating 'the nation' – both as an abstract ideal, and the Italian and German nations in particular. Such cultural production can be seen as a key part of 'romanticism' (a movement that swept Europe in the period 1775–1830, the aims of which included a return to nature, a belief in the goodness of humanity, the development of nationalistic pride and the exaltation of the senses and emotions over reason and intellect). Consider, for example, the following fragment of Johann Gottlieb Fichte's *Addresses to the German Nation*. These addresses were written in 1807–08 and delivered in Berlin when, as detailed in Unit 17, the whole of Europe was threatened by Napoleonic expansion.

> The first, original and truly natural frontiers of all states are undoubtedly their inner frontiers. Those who speak the same language are linked together, before human intervention takes a hand, by mere nature with a host of invisible ties; they understand each other and are capable of communicating more and more closely with one another, they belong together, they are by nature one indivisible whole. No other nation of a different origin and language can try to appropriate and absorb such a people without becoming confused itself in the first place, or without disturbing profoundly the uniform progress of its own education.
>
> [...]
>
> Our present problem ... is simply to preserve the existence and community of what is German. All other differences vanish before this higher point of view ... It is essential that the higher love of Fatherland, for the entire people of the German nation, reign supreme, and justly so, in every particular German state.
>
> (Quoted in Snyder, 1964, pp. 164–5)

You can see clearly here that a distinction is being made between the German 'state' and the German cultural 'nation'. However, there is little doubt that nationalists like Fichte sought to inculcate a sense of oneness, of German national identity, across existing political borders. While no country called Germany yet existed, 'German' national identity is depicted as worthy of struggle and possessing a virtue before all others. See Figure 19.3 for another example of German romanticism.

[handwritten margin note: intellectuals leading the 'Romantic' movement.]

Figure 19.3   Caspar David Friedrich, *The Oak Tree in the Snow*, 1829, oil on canvas, 71 x 48 cm.
Nationalgalerie, Staatlichen Museen, Berlin. Photo: © BPK/Nationalgalerie, SMB/Jörg P. Anders.
Friedrich was one of the main proponents of German romanticism. This painting is both
naturalistic and allegorical. As well as conveying love of the natural world, the German oak
represented here also symbolises the German people. Although dead branches speak of a lost
past, new life springs at the roots and the blue sky hints at regeneration. The oak tree was a
symbol charged with nationalist sentiment in Germany.

In Italy, too, support for the national ideal often came from poets and scholars. Reproduced below is an extract from a work by the Italian poet and patriot Ugo Foscolo, also produced in 1807.

> Italy! O lovely land! O temple of Venus and of the Muses! How thou art portrayed by travellers who make a show of honouring thee! How thou art humiliated by foreigners who have the presumption to seek to master thee! But who can depict thee better than he who is destined to see thy beauty all his life long? ... Neither the barbarity of the Goths, nor the internal civic struggles, the devastation of many campaigns, the denunciations of theologians, nor the monopoly of learning by the clergy, could suffice to quench the immortal fire that animated the Etruscans [a pre-Roman people] and the Latins, that fired Dante's immortal spirit amidst the sufferings of his exile, Machiavelli in the anguish of his torture, Galileo among the terrors of the Inquisition ... unquenchable the fire not in these alone, but in countless other noble souls who suffered disaster and poverty in silence. Prostrate upon their tombs, ask the secret of their greatness ... and how their love of fatherland, of glory and of truth increased their constancy of heart, their strength of mind and the benefits they have conferred upon us.
> (Quoted in Snyder, 1964, p. 81)

This extract is perhaps a little harder to interpret than the straightforward call for solidarity penned by Fichte. However, clearly this is again a celebration of 'Italy' – despite the fact that no such political entity as yet existed. There is a clear sense of pride in perceived past glory (particularly the Roman empire) and also a sense that this past greatness can be recreated through unity and struggle in the present. So, one element in the rise of national sentiment in Europe during the nineteenth century may well have been the spread of new ideas (which, inversely, often harked back to a former, mythical period of unity) celebrating a national solidarity that did not yet exist. However, it is important to note that these depictions of national glory remained primarily *cultural* in the early part of the nineteenth century. While it was obviously significant that artists and thinkers began to concern themselves with 'the nation' (see Figure 19.4), it took a lot of hard dealing, political wrangling and strong-arm tactics before the putative 'nations' of Italy and Germany became unified nation states.

In the case of Italy, the process of unification came to be known as the *Risorgimento* (resurrection) after the journal *Il Risorgimento*, published from the end of 1847 in Turin by Cesare Balbo. As well as setting up publications such as this, *Risorgimento* nationalists created political organisations – associations of groups and individuals with shared aims. There was such a wide range of nationalist organisations that it is not really possible to speak of *the* national movement in Italy. Rather, different organisations had different agendas and visions of Italy. Some held public meetings, ran in elections, petitioned parliament and attempted to hold 'national' festivals. Others took the form of secret societies and paramilitary organisations that were prepared

Figure 19.4   Raffaelle Monti, *The Sleep of Sorrow and the Dream of Joy, An Allegory of the Italian Risorgimento*, 1861, carved marble. Victoria & Albert Museum, London. Photo: V&A Images

to use force and break the law. Such organisations called on fellow Italians to achieve unity by violent means if necessary. The Carbonari, for example, one such secret society, proclaimed in underground literature in 1817 – 'To arms, then! To arms! Let your battle-word be the love of your country and compassion for your offspring [...] He alone is worthy of life who loves his country' (Rath, 1964, p. 359). Giuseppe Mazzini's Giovine Italia (Young Italy), formed in Marseilles in 1831, also set up numerous revolutionary cells throughout the Italian peninsular, all pushing for change. These participated in the revolutions of 1848, but many gains made during this period were lost again, partly due to Austrian intervention.

Popular revolutionary organisations such as Young Italy did have a key role to play in generating public support for the nationalist project. However, one of the names most closely associated with Italian unification is that of Count Camillo di Cavour, who became prime minister of Sardinia in 1852. His hard-headed power politics were crucial to the eventual success of the unification project. Cavour met with Napoleon III of France and persuaded him to assent to a secretly planned war against Austria, the upshot of which was that the Austrians were forced to surrender Lombardy – which Napoleon eventually ceded to Victor Emmanuel II, the king of Piedmont. After this, all of the northern states joined the kingdom of Sardinia between 1859 and 1861 (you may wish to have another look at Figures 19.1 and 19.2 at this point). The role of another forceful nationalist, Giuseppe Garibaldi should also be cited here (see Figure 19.5). He is initially noteworthy for his heroic deeds as a military leader of nationalist forces in the unsuccessful war against Austria after 1848. Later, however, Garibaldi's dream of a united Italy motivated his successful expedition against the Austrian forces in the Alps in 1859. In 1860, he conquered Sicily and set up a provisional insular government. Garibaldi then conquered Naples, which he delivered to Victor Emmanuel in 1861. With the annexation of Umbria and Marches from the papal government, a united Italy was finally established in 1861 with Victor Emmanuel as its king. Venice was added to Italy in 1866 after Prussia defeated Austria in the Seven Weeks' War, in which Italy sided with Prussia; Venice was its reward. Then, in 1870, during the Franco-Prussian War, Napoleon III withdrew his troops from Rome. With the city of Rome and the remaining Papal States left unprotected, Italian troops moved into Rome without opposition. The pope refused to recognise the legitimacy of the new government, and hence was confined to the Vatican (which even today remains a state in and of itself). Rome voted for union with Italy in October 1870 and, in July 1871, Rome became the capital of a united Italy.

In the case of Germany, the success of the unification project can again be attributed to a similar mix of new ideas, political pressure and strong-arm tactics. As regards ideas, among the most significant were the philosophical writings of Gottfried Herder.

Figure 19.5   Brog, Guiseppe Garibaldi (1807–1882), photograph. Photo: Mary Evans Picture Library

Now read Anthology Document 5.23 – an extract from Herder's *Materials for the Philosophy of the History of Mankind*, written in 1784. Once you have read it, answer the following questions. What, for Herder, are the key components of national identity? What do you think Herder might have to say about the possibility of changing one's national identity?

Spend about 30 minutes on this exercise.

Herder sees national identity as something entirely natural in human beings. As he notes, 'nature brings forth families; the most natural state therefore is also one people, with a national character of its own'. Language is, for Herder, a key component of this national character. He argues that particular languages are vital to particular national cultures. He implies that different languages lead individuals to think and feel in particular ways that are unique to their own 'people'. As such, we can surmise that Herder would have believed it impossible for an individual to change his nationality.

Herder was writing in Riga (a German-speaking city in Latvia), and was reflecting on the value of the local Lettish culture, which he felt was being suppressed by the growing cosmopolitanism of his time. He was uneasy that educated Germans were keen to speak French (which was fashionable at the time) rather than their native tongue. His vision of nationalism is therefore primarily cultural. Because he saw the world as divided naturally into different peoples or national cultures, and because he believed that a people could only thrive when it used its own language to express a national culture, he thought that rulers should allow diverse peoples to speak their own languages and enjoy their own cultures. As he noted, 'no greater injury can be inflicted on a nation than to be robbed of her national character, the peculiarity of her spirit and her language'. Perhaps you noted that there is no real connection between national identity and political or state forms in Herder's writings. Nationalism, for him, does not have connotations of rivalry. Provided rulers allow 'peoples' to have their own national cultures Herder is not concerned with who governs whom. Therefore, it is difficult to decide just how important thinkers such as Herder were in the unification of Germany.

While an influential factor, German unification was not simply the result of an upsurge of patriotism among a population reading romantic philosophy and suddenly realising the unity between themselves. Rather, as in Italy, gradual pressure on the part of activist organisations, a number of false starts, and some decisive action on the part of key individuals were vital. After the Congress of Vienna, the thirty-nine independent German states differed greatly in size and were divided both politically and economically. All were subject to a great deal of Austrian influence, which was hostile to integration. While nationalism gradually gained currency in intellectual circles, the king of Prussia (the most powerful German state), Frederick William III, was more concerned with preserving Prussian power than with unification – especially if unification entailed a constitution. By 1834, however, most German states had joined a customs union known as the *Zollverein*, and in 1838 a single currency was adopted. As in Italy, some gains were made following the 1848 revolutions, but eventually Frederick William IV of Prussia and the other German princes were able to re-establish the status quo. Over the next two

decades, however, Prussia increased in power and, through skilled negotiation
on the part of Otto von Bismarck (the Prussian prime minister) as well as wars
with Denmark (1864), Austria (1866) and France (1870–1), Prussia enticed or
forced the other states to join Prussia in a united Germany under the Prussian
King Wilhelm I, who was proclaimed German *Kaiser* (emperor) on 18 January
1871. (in Paris) ∼Versailles∼

So, the unifications of Italy and Germany can be at least partly attributed to a
mix of new ideas in the air, the spread of political and cultural organisations
promoting these ideas, revolutionary struggles and decisive action on the part
of a number of key political players. There is obviously not space to consider
here the many other successful national movements of the nineteenth century.
However, despite considerable local differences, most do demonstrate this
pattern of a distinct wave of cultural and philosophical enthusiasm for the
'nation', the growth of popular pressure (at least on the part of certain classes)
and decisive action by a number of determined political activists. These were
undoubtedly exciting times. Enthusiasm for the principle that oppressed
peoples should govern themselves was infectious. The English poet Lord
Byron, for example, was so impressed by the Greek struggle for independence
after centuries of rule by the Ottoman empire that he travelled (with a great
deal of ceremony) to Greece to assist in the struggle. Unfortunately, he died
from fever shortly after arrival, in 1824.

However, as outlined in the introduction, the formation of nation states is
rarely (if ever) a clean, clear-cut process. Certainly in the cases of both
Germany and Italy, while nationalists depicted the processes of unification as
the inexorable dawning of the notion of the right to sovereignty of 'the
people', this notion has to be deconstructed somewhat. National unity does not
necessarily exist just because politicians proclaim unification. As Lucy Riall
has noted in the case of Italy:

> Liberalism and nationalism's victorious moment in 1860 was,
> however, short-lived and Italian unification came to disappoint those
> who had celebrated it so loudly. The death in June 1861 of Italy's first
> prime minister Camillo Cavour, regarded as the architect of national
> unity, seems in retrospect to have closed definitively the 'heroic'
> phase of the Risorgimento.
>
> (Riall, 1993, p. 46)

More specifically, there was a crisis of legitimacy in southern Italy, the church
refused to recognise the kingdom of Italy and there was widespread resentment
in many parts of Italy at the heavy-handed way in which administrative unity
was imposed in the four years after 1861. In Germany, too, the picture was not
entirely rosy following unification. To start with, the empire formed in 1871
was not a 'Great Germany', encompassing all Germans. Outside its frontiers,
in Switzerland, Austria and Bohemia in particular, were still millions of
individuals who considered themselves German. This periodically caused
tension both inside and outside Germany. In Austria during the 1880s, for
example, a pan-German movement led by Georg von Schönerer agitated for

the unification of the German-speaking parts of the Habsburg empire with
Germany proper. Equally, within Germany there were divisions. Bavarians, for
example, largely considered themselves Bavarian first and German second, and
regional rivalries continued long after 1871, as Bavaria, Würtemburg, Saxony
and Prussia all maintained separate armies. The Polish minority within
Germany, too, often felt alienated from the new Reich (empire) and were
mistrusted by Bismarck, who feared their concentration in the provinces that
were most likely to be attacked by Russia in the event of war. Various anti-
Polish measures were introduced. In 1886, for example, the Settlement Law
provided over 100 million marks to Germans who were willing to buy up
Polish-owned land in the east, and helped to broker the sales. At the same
time, measures were introduced to suppress the Polish language and to ensure
education took place only in German. Despite this, as Seligman and McLean
note, 'The main legacy of the anti-Polish policies pursued by Bismarck and the
Prussian government in the 1870s and 1880s was greater unity among Prussian
Poles, and a stronger sense of alienation among them from the Prussian state
and the Reich' (Seligman and McLean, 2000, p. 25).

Thus, although there was undoubtedly a large measure of popular enthusiasm
for the rise of new nation states in Europe during the nineteenth century, even
towards the end of the century most countries were still very different from the
nation states we know today. The social life of many nineteenth-century states
was marked by linguistic divisions, by the tensions precipitated by
discontented minorities who felt disadvantaged by redrawing of Europe's
boundaries, by regional identities that were more important to many than their
national affiliation and by sectarian religious divisions, which again were more
significant in the lives of many than any putative national unity. Some
successful nation states, such as Belgium and Switzerland, were based on
creating nations that defied linguistic, and perhaps even cultural, unity.
Moreover, even in existing nation states, such as France and Britain, national
unity was far from certain. It is wrong to assume that by the mid nineteenth
century all inhabitants of given country felt a strong sense of unity with one
another (see Figure 19.6). We have already touched on the case of France
above, and I would like you now to consider the development of national
identity in France in a little more detail.

EXERCISE

I would like you to read two secondary source extracts, which you can find on the
A200 website. The first is from a seminal work on French history, Eugen Weber's
Peasants into Frenchmen. The Modernization of Rural France, 1870–1914 (pp.
95–114). The second is the first few pages of an article discussing regional identity
in France – 'The nation in the village' by Peter Sahlins (read up to the end of the
paragraph beginning 'Peasants, artisans, and notables ...').You do not have to read
the whole article, but of course you may if you wish. Jot down some answers in note
form to the following three questions.

- What are the main points that each author makes about regional and national
  identities in France?

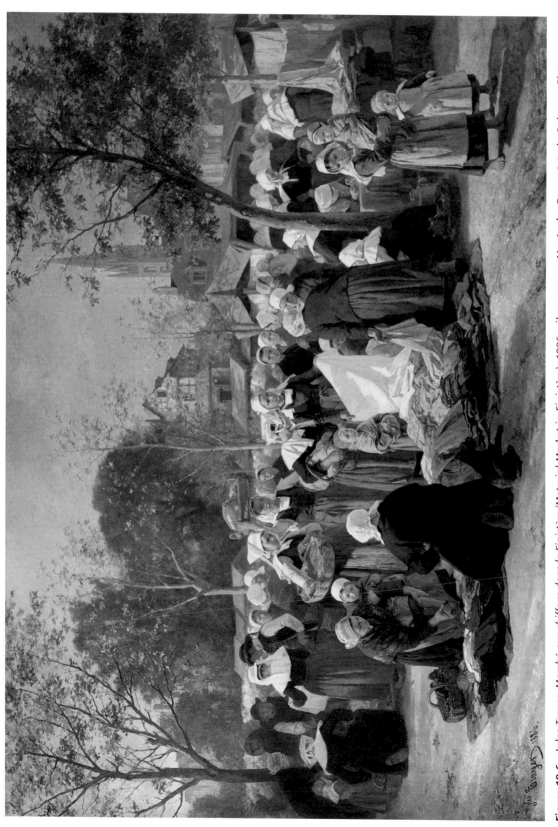

Figure 19.6 Jules Trayer, *Marché aux chiffons dans le Finistère* (Material Market in Finistère), 1886, oil on canvas. Musée des Beaux-Arts de Quimper. Photo: Giraudon/ The Bridgeman Art Library. This work by Trayer shows the significance of regional culture in France, with its distinctive modes of dress and trade specialities, until late in the nineteenth century

- Can you tell to what period each author attributes the decisive development of French national identity?
- What are some of the factors that stand in the way of a homogenous national identity?

There is no need to write out formal answers to these questions, but do take plenty of notes as you read. Making notes and underlining key phrases will help you get into the habit of reading academic publications effectively.

Spend about 45 minutes on this exercise.

SPECIMEN ANSWER

Weber's main thesis is that, even in the second half of the nineteenth century, when many might have assumed that France was an entirely coherent nation, it was in fact 'very incompletely integrated'. Those living in outlying regions of France, particularly in areas such as Brittany, which had a very distinct regional culture, were very late to invest much significance in their membership of the French nation. As evidence of this, Weber cites attitudes towards the Franco-Prussian War of 1870/71, arguing that many local populations (although initially enthusiastic) quickly became indifferent to the struggle. It was only later in the century (the period 1880–1920, specifically) that the state actively used educational methods to inculcate a sense of 'Frenchness' in the bulk of the population.

Sahlins nuances this picture somewhat through a study of the Cerdanya, a region in the Pyrenees on the border between France and Spain, where a vibrant Catalan language and culture co-existed with French and Spanish national identities. In the introduction to the article, Sahlins makes it clear, first, that some 'national' sentiment existed in the region before the period to which Weber attributes significance and, second, that even when the French state attempted to inculcate national sentiment 'from the top down' during the nineteenth century, this did not entirely erode regional Catalan identities.

DISCUSSION

In another work, Sahlins cites the *Hymn of Cerdanya*, written in the late 1890s and sung in Catalan, which encapsulates this duality well:

> We are the heirs of the mountain
> we are the sons of the Pyrenees,
> sons of France or of Spain,
> we are all brothers at Font Romeu.
> Here is our cradle and our tombstone
> Which is our natural patria;
> From the Carlit to the Tossa
> From the Cadi to the Puigmal.
> Half of France, half of Spain
> there is no land like the Cerdanya.

(Sahlins, 1991, p. 228)

Evoking a local pride of place, the song describes a set of 'natural frontiers' of the patria that fail to accord with the political division of the valley between France and Spain. Both regional and national identities continued to have significance in the Cerdanya, co-existed side by side and were pressed into service as different situations demanded.

Thus, even in long-established nation states, an investigation of national
sentiment and national identity during the nineteenth century throws up
contradictory evidence. One thing that can be stated with certainty, however, is
that by the end of the nineteenth century most of the nation states discussed in
this section were far more coherent than at the beginning. The drawing
together of nation states was a gradual process that involved a number of
variables. Governments, as Weber notes, could implement educational
programmes designed to instil a sense of pride in their specific national
histories (something that will be discussed in more detail in Unit 20). States
could also enforce linguistic codes, make trade simpler within national
boundaries, and link up outlying regions with road and rail networks. All these
factors gradually helped individuals to feel more of a connection with the
nation state in which they lived – whether it was centuries old or of more
recent advent. Newspapers became widely available by the end of the
nineteenth century and, again, helped to convey a sense of unity among
populations reading about the same events in the same language, often for the
first time. By the start of the twentieth century, national sentiment was clearly
one of the most significant elements in western European social life. In a
number of eastern states, the picture was somewhat more complex, but
unfortunately there is not sufficient space to investigate this here. Many
historians have sought to understand and to explain the reasons for such a
significant change in popular consciousness, and for the rest of the unit we will
be considering and comparing some of these explanations.

THE 'MODERNITY' OF NATION STATES

The formation of the nation states of Europe is a phenomenon that has
interested historians from the nineteenth century onwards. In fact, it might be
argued that early historians had an influential role to play in the very
development of nation states during the period, often intentionally seeking to
glorify the mythical past of their own particular nation state rather than
considering the process in the abstract. This is something which we will be
moving on to consider in a bit more detail in Unit 20. Indeed, until well into
the twentieth century historians generally remained very uncritical of the rise
of nation states, and mostly believed the rhetoric espoused by nationalists – of
the glorious flowering of national unity, the struggle to recover long-past glory
and so forth.

However, from the 1960s onwards, historians (and social scientists, who also
became very interested in nationalism) began to devise a series of ever more
sophisticated explanations for why national identity became so fundamental to
the way we live today. We will consider below the work of Ernest Gellner,
John Breuilly, Eric Hobsbawm and Benedict Anderson. Given that national
identity had not always been an important matter, and that for hundreds of
years most people acquiesced to be governed by rulers who did not necessarily
speak their language or share their culture, many of the recent explanations put
forward for the rise of nation states and national identity have focused on their

'modernity'. In other words, historians have recently tended to see nations and nationalism as phenomena connected with the rise of the modern, industrial societies that characterise Europe today, rather than as something 'intrinsic' or naturally present in human nature, as had previously often been assumed.

You may recall that you have already encountered one of the most influential theories addressing the 'modernity' or otherwise of nation states. The work of Ernest Gellner was touched on in Unit 18 and earlier in this unit. Gellner argued, essentially, that nation states are intrinsically *modern* and indeed only became *possible* with the rise of industrial societies. In the feudal past, according to Gellner, cultures had often been largely *horizontal*. That is to say, the languages and cultures of the ruling elites and those they ruled were often quite separate, particularly in large multinational empires. Because life during these times was 'a difficult and serious business', all that peasants required was protection and freedom from oppression (Gellner, 1983, p. 153). All that those who ruled them required was the delivery of food and produce. Effective government was thus all that mattered. The notion that those who ruled should be of the same nationality as the mass of the population would have appeared as a 'curious frivolity'. However, clearly, something had happened to change this situation. What had made 'the once frivolous question about the language or culture of rulers paramount'? The answer, for Gellner, was modernisation.

Gellner argued that, during feudal, agrarian periods, the culture of most populations was both localised and very rigidly structured. People did not normally travel far from their villages or towns, and much of their daily life relied on knowledge of local customs and familiarity with those who lived nearby. With the coming of industrialisation, however, this changed. The greater social mobility that industrial society entailed meant that social relations now had to be 'portable'. In other words, education could no longer be supplied at the village or even regional level. With individuals migrating long distances to larger towns and cities in search of work, a bigger, more uniform education system was required to enable individuals to communicate and work effectively with one another. Only *states* had the resources to supply appropriate education. By gaining a monopoly over education (and by teaching a single language, a single history, and so forth), modern industrial states therefore *created* nations (rather than the other way around). Thus, for Gellner, 'nationalism is not the awakening of nations to self-consciousness: it invents nations where they do not exist'. As he summarised:

> nationalism is an essential component of modernisation, or the transition from agrarian to industrial society – the latter requiring a state that can produce and be maintained by one common, literate and accessible culture.
>
> (Quoted in O'Leary, 1997, p. 198)

Gellner was, of course, aware that his theory was 'highly schematised and simplified' and claimed that it was only intended to capture 'the general underlying pattern of modern nationalism'. However, concentrating as it does primarily on *economic* factors, it has been criticised on a number of grounds.

[margin handwritten notes: Gellner stresses economic factors]

[margin handwritten notes: modernisation thru industrialisation meant basics couldn't be guaranteed at regional level.]

Perhaps you have already spotted one problem with Gellner's theory as outlined above? There does not seem to be a neat relationship between industrialisation and the processes Gellner describes. In France, for example, unified educational provision was introduced towards the end of the nineteenth century, significantly *after* the main period of industrialisation. That said, Gellner's theory does point us in some interesting directions. His focus on the importance of state education in relation to national identity is thought provoking, and I would like you to explore this aspect in a little more detail below.

EXERCISE

Now read Anthology Document 5.24, 'Extracts from a range of Third Republic primary and secondary school textbooks', printed during the French Third Republic (1870–1940). As you read the extracts, consider the following question – What do you think would be the likely effect on a French child of reading such works from a very early age?

Spend about 20 minutes on this exercise.

SPECIMEN ANSWER

Clearly, these textbooks are portraying a very specific view of France to children. Words used to describe France include 'powerful', 'respected', 'historic' and 'greatest'. An image of 'France', which after all is a fairly abstract entity, is presented that seems to demand respect and devotion. France is also described as having a certain 'role' in the world. The textbooks argue that the French Revolution has shown the people of France the importance of self-government and imply that the French, therefore, have a duty to spread these ideas overseas through a 'civilising mission' (something you will encounter in the next block). These textbooks seem (and indeed were) specifically designed to elicit a two-fold response from children. First, there are numerous exhortations to 'love' France, which is depicted as entirely worthy of this love. Second, children are urged to do their 'duty' when France calls – whatever that duty might be (the defence of France in a war and the export of French ideas to the colonies are both mentioned). We can see clearly that there is continuity in these textbooks from the primary level upwards. It seems very unlikely that children could have received this type of instruction over a course of years without it having had at least *some* impact on the way in which they came to view the country in which they lived. Far from national identity being a naturally occurring phenomenon, these extracts appear to indicate that education and socialisation probably have a very strong role to play in the type of identity we assume as adults.

DISCUSSION

Although the extracts under consideration here are from France, a selection of English or German school textbooks would reveal very similar themes. You may have noticed that some of the phrases used in the textbooks have almost a quasi-religious feel. Many authors have argued that national sentiment has distinct similarities with religious sentiment, particularly during the nineteenth century. As participation in organised religion declined during the nineteenth century, the 'love' and 'devotion' previously allocated to the church came to be directed towards the nations in which individuals lived. The pioneering sociologist Emile Durkheim believed that religious rituals and national rituals (such as the singing of national anthems) had many similarities, and argued that 'it is by uttering the same cry, pronouncing the same word, or performing the same gesture in regard to some object that they [the people] become and feel themselves to be in unison' (Guibernau, 1996, p. 27).

Thus the spread of state-sponsored education may well have been an important factor in the development of national sentiment during the nineteenth century. Gellner did not refer specifically to this type of 'patriotic' education, but rather concerned himself more with the idea that a common education system in a common language gives individuals a feeling of community that they do not share with those from abroad. This aside, his ideas about industrialisation *requiring* a certain type of education system, which in turn led to the development of national sentiment, are convincing to a degree. However, some historians believe that Gellner sets too much store by one single factor (industrialisation) and have sought to augment this purely *economic* argument with theories that focus instead on the political or cultural aspects of nationalism. For example, where Gellner stressed economic factors as vital in the development of nation states, John Breuilly has concentrated on politics, arguing that, rather than focusing on industrialisation, 'nationalism is best understood as an especially appropriate form of *political* behaviour in the context of the modern state and the modern state system' (Breuilly, 1993, p. 1).

Breuilly chooses "political behaviour"

In common with Gellner, Breuilly's starting point is that nationalism does not represent or spring from a spontaneous upsurge of 'national identity', although it is an intrinsically *modern* phenomenon. However, unlike Gellner, he believes it is not a good idea to look for 'deep', structural factors (such as economic development or modernisation) that explain nationalism. Rather, for Breuilly, nationalism is always about politics, politics is always about power, and power is always really about control of the state (see Figure 19.7). While the rapid urbanisation and industrialisation of the nineteenth century did lead to massive changes in existing social relations, this did not *on its own* lead to nationalism. What was required for modern nationalism to develop was for the possibility of a new form of identity and politics to be seized upon by different groups seeking power, and for the intellectual discourse of the time to be turned into a nationalist ideology and rhetoric by a process of simplification, repetition and the dissemination of symbols and ceremonies. In other words, it is not the new ideas that intellectuals promote, or the fact that people are receptive to these new ideas, that are important in the rise of nationalism; what is significant is the political commitment and organisation of key individuals, who take advantage of this situation to bid for power. Therefore, as Breuilly summarises:

> the key to a general understanding of nationalism is to be found in the sphere of political action and organisation. That is **not** to say that politics is more important than social interests and ideology in any or indeed all particular cases. It is only to argue that the search for the common features underlying all nationalist movements should focus upon the political context.
>
> (Breuilly, 1993, p. 72)

Breuilly contends that it is not ideas or economic changes which are really important to the formation of nation states, but rather the political opportunities which these new ideas and changes make possible. As you will recall from earlier in this unit, the actions of nationalist politicians such as

Figure 19.7 'The voting papers on unification with Sardinia are given in Naples', Plebiscite 21 October 1860, engraving after a drawing by Konrad Gross, from *Illustrierte Zeitung*, vol. 35, no.908, 24 November 1860. Photo: AKG, London. The possibilities of the plebiscite as a device for the legitimising of aggression and despoliation were discovered by politicians in the nineteenth century. In 1860, a plebiscite launched the new Italian state. Ten years later, a plebiscite sanctioned the seizure of Rome

Cavour, Garibaldi and Bismarck were vital in the securing the unifications of Italy and Germany, and such evidence does seem to support Breuilly's arguments. That said, Breuilly (like Gellner) has been criticised for providing too *monocausal* an investigation of nationalism – in other words, for focusing solely on *one* key factor to the exclusion of others. Some authors have argued that a focus on politics (or indeed on the economy, as in the case of Gellner) does not explain the deep passions that nationalism seemed able to raise in many European populations during the nineteenth century. Historians such as Eric Hobsbawm and Benedict Anderson have claimed that it is important also to consider the *cultural* and *social* aspects of the rise of nation states. Only by linking these with earlier economic and political explanations, they argue, can a more rounded theory of nationalism be produced.

Eric Hobsbawm, for example, contended that explanations of the rise of nation states that focus solely on the impersonal forces of modernisation (Gellner) or solely on the desire for power of elites (Breuilly) can never be fully satisfactory. Rather, he argued, nationalism 'cannot be understood unless also analysed from below, that is in terms of the assumptions, hopes, needs, longings and interests of ordinary people' (Hobsbawm, 1990, p. 10). Hobsbawm believed that the rapid industrialisation and urbanisation of the late eighteenth and nineteenth centuries broke down existing social structures and gave rise to a need for new forms of identity. In other words, if an individual's identity was no longer focused on the familiar local traditions of a specific village or region (perhaps because he/she had recently moved to the anonymity of a big new town or city), that individual would develop a *need* for something to provide a sense of social stability and security in their life. At the same time, however, Hobsbawm went on to analyse the rise of the modern centralised state during the nineteenth century. The modern bureaucratic state was novel partly because it ruled its citizens directly (rather than through regional princes or outlying aristocrats), and partly because it had to take account of the wishes of its populace to a greater degree than ever before. This might have been the case either because they now had an electoral voice, or because the state needed their practical consent or activity in other ways, such as conscription or tax collection. As such, he argued: 'states and regimes had every reason to reinforce, if they could, state patriotism with the sentiments and symbols of "imagined community", wherever and however they originated, and to concentrate them upon themselves' (Hobsbawm, 1990, p. 91).

He explored a number of examples of the ways in which the new bureaucratic states of the nineteenth century sought to foster patriotism (national pride) in their citizens. We have already discussed education above, but Hobsbawm also analysed the spread of commemorative holidays (Bastille Day, for example, commemorating the French Revolution of 1789, in fact dates from 1880 – see Figure 19.8), the issue of historical stamps, the building of war memorials, and the use of national flags and anthems, all of which acted to provide the sense of identity individuals craved in their new, fluid industrial societies. Overall, then, Hobsbawm presented a picture of nationalism as a multifaceted

à Paris chez D. Mourgue ... Édit.

Rue St Jacques 22

ARCHIVES NATIONALES
MUSÉE DE L'HISTOIRE DE FRANCE

LA RÉPUBLIQUE TRIOMPHANTE PRÉSIDE A LA GRANDE FÊTE NATIONALE DU 14 JUILLET 1880
Distribution des Drapeaux. — Anniversaire de la prise de la Bastille. (14 Juillet 1789)

Figure 19.8 La République Triomphante Préside A La Grande Fête Nationale Du 14 Juillet 1880 (The triumphant republic celebrates the national holiday of 14 July 1880) – commemorating the storming of the Bastille during the French Revolution. Centre Historique des Archives Nationales, Paris. Photo: CHAN. Bastille Day only became a national holiday in France in 1880, and the 'Marseillaise' was only adopted as the national anthem in the same year

construction – something that satisfied both the needs of elites and the modern state as well as the desires and practices of their newly enfranchised populations.

Another important work, Benedict Anderson's *Imagined Communities*, also sought to emphasise the role of cultural factors in the construction of nationalism, and to explain why it had the power to produce such an emotional response in individuals. Anderson's work is complex but insightful. Take your time reading the next couple of paragraphs. Thinking of the First World War, he pondered – 'what makes the shrunken imaginings of recent history (scarcely more than two centuries) generate such colossal sacrifices?' (Anderson, 1991, p. 7). He concluded that, while nationalism is an intrinsically modern phenomenon, it is its 'deep' cultural heritage which explains both its success and its longevity. Nationalism can best be understood, he argued, 'by aligning it, not with self-consciously held political ideologies, but with the large cultural systems that preceded it, out of which ... it came into being' (Anderson, 1991, p. 12). For Anderson, the historical setting for the rise of nationalism was initially framed by the simultaneous decline of religious 'world views' and of dynastic realms based on divine right. This dual process gave rise to the need for a secular agency to provide meaning in life and a sense of continuity after death. The relevance of this to the themes of beliefs and ideologies should be readily apparent. However, it is far too simplistic simply to state that as religious world views declined, people transferred their allegiance to the new nation states.

Rather, Anderson argues that, at this crucial juncture, history was marked by the 'crossing' of three very specific historical forces – the invention of print technology, the development of capitalism, and the 'fatal diversity of human language'. Initially, print capitalism produced books for the Latin-reading market. However, this limited market was rapidly saturated with books, and a capitalist imperative arose to seek out new vernacular (local) linguistic markets. It was obviously unprofitable to publish books in every local dialect or linguistic variant, and hence a streamlining process was necessary, which involved the selection of certain majority 'print languages'. This process had a three-fold impact. In the first place, it 'created unified fields of exchange and communication below Latin and above spoken vernaculars' (Anderson, 1991, p. 44). This meant not only that speakers of variants of (for example) French or English who would have had trouble communicating in person could henceforth comprehend each other through print, but also that they gradually became aware that they were linked to thousands of individuals in this way, and similarly differentiated from others. In addition, the process of streamlining gave a new fixity to languages, which helped to build the image of antiquity so vital to the nation. Finally, it created 'languages-of-power of a kind different from the older administrative vernaculars' (Anderson, 1991, p. 44). In other words, some dialectic variants were relegated to the margins of society, while others became more mainstream, and more closely associated with secular power. The combination of all the above historical factors gradually made possible the 'imagination' of the nation in an unprecedented way. Returning to his notion of the widespread attachment of peoples to the 'inventions of their imaginations', Anderson concluded that this could only be explained by an analysis of the deep cultural roots of the nation as an 'imagined community', one which provided an impression of continuity beyond death and a sense of 'place' unavailable to any other type of organisation.

These are just a few of the very many explanations that have been provided for the rise of nation states and nationalism during the eighteenth and nineteenth centuries. Some focus primarily on the economic changes associated with the period, some on the political sphere and others on the social and cultural changes associated with the rise of nation states (Lawrence, 2004). Perhaps you already find one type of explanation more convincing than the others. It seems likely that all of these theories have something to offer those of us trying to understand the rise of nationalism. That said, each has its own flaws and it is unlikely that any one theory can convincingly explain all aspects of this puzzling phenomenon. In particular, each of the theories discussed above identifies nationalism as primarily a *modern* phenomenon, and dates the rise of recognisable nation states in Europe to the eighteenth and nineteenth centuries. However, there are historians who date the rise, or at least the roots, of nation states much earlier than this, and it is the work of these historians that will be the subject of the third section of this unit.

'WHEN' IS A NATION?

Most of the analysis discussed in the previous section was concerned with those historians and social scientists who believe that both nationalism and nation states are *modern*, intrinsically linked to the rise of industrial societies in Europe from the eighteenth century onwards. While they focus on different explanatory variables, this approach as a whole is sometimes referred to as 'classical modernism' (Lawrence, 2004). As we have seen, there is much to commend these explanations of nationalism. However, as usual, not all historians agree. You will recall that earlier in the course you came across arguments for a sense of national identity in, variously, fourteenth-century Normandy, sixteenth-century Netherlands, and Scotland and Ireland in the seventeenth century. However, this shorter third section of this unit will consider some of contrasting viewpoints and evidence presented by Adrian Hastings, Liah Greenfeld and Anthony Smith. The title of this section '"When" is a nation?' is taken from a thought-provoking article by the American political scientist Walker Connor (Connor, 1990). Given that nations do not suddenly spring into being, he posed the interesting question of how we can tell at what point in their development they come to warrant the title of 'nation'?

Many of the theorists of 'classical modernism' (proposing the notion of the 'modernity' of nation states and nationalism) were themselves historians of the modern period, or social scientists with a less than comprehensive knowledge of history. The challenge to 'classical modernism' has come from two camps.

In the first place, some specialists in the medieval and early modern periods have argued that they can identify recognisable 'national' sentiment long before the onset of industrialisation and modernisation. In the second place, a group of scholars led by Anthony Smith have contended that it is impossible to understand the form and significance of modern nation states without some consideration of the deeper ethnic roots that lie behind them.

Turning first to the work of medievalists and early modernists, scholars such as Adrian Hastings and Liah Greenfeld believe that it is entirely possible to locate (in England in particular) some form of national sentiment long before the onset of modernity. Hastings, for example, notes that 'social scientists enter the Middle Ages at their peril', and sought to use his detailed knowledge of the period to prove that national consciousness could be discerned as early as the twelfth century, although its strongest expressions are seen in and after the sixteenth century. As he claimed, 'if nationalism became theoretically central to western political thinking in the nineteenth century, it existed as a powerful reality in some places long before that' (Hastings, 1997, p. 4).

Hastings focuses much of his attention on England, as do other scholars writing in a similar vein, believing it to be the first recognisable European nation. Indeed, he noted that, 'it is odd that historians of nationalism have managed for long so easily to avert their eyes from what in hard reality, I believe, has been the prototype for the whole story' (Hastings, 1997, p. 6). He engaged with the modernism of Hobsbawm in particular. Where the latter had used the definitions found in dictionaries of the nineteenth century in support of his claim that our understanding of the word 'nation' was a recent development, Hastings countered that 'the frequency and consistency in usage of the word from the early fourteenth century onward strongly suggests a basis in experience: Englishmen felt themselves to be a nation' (Hastings, 1997, p. 15). Even Bede's *Ecclesiastical History of the English People*, Hastings claimed, written in about AD 730, took for granted the existence of a 'single nation'. England served as a prototype or exemplar, and the twin processes of the development of vernacular literatures and the consolidation of modern states served to facilitate the permeation of the model throughout Europe. Overall, for Hastings, there is thus very little relationship between nation formation and nationalism, and modernity. Rather, 'only when modernisation was itself already in the air did they almost accidentally become part of it, in particular from the eighteenth century when the political and economic success of England made it a model to imitate' (Hastings, 1997, p. 205).

Liah Greenfeld has also focused on England as an exemplar in the field of nations, and as the first nation in the pre-modern period. Considering the genesis of the 'idea' of the nation, she concluded:

> At a certain point in history – to be precise, in early sixteenth-century England – the word 'nation' in its conciliar meaning of 'an elite' was applied to the population of the country and made synonymous with the word 'people'. This semantic transformation signalled the

emergence of the first nation in the world, in the sense in which the word is understood today, and launched the era of nationalism.

(Greenfeld, 1992, p. 6)

She went on to make even stronger claims regarding the link between nations and modernity. Not only did the advent of the nation precede modernity, but, in fact, the idea of the nation formed 'the constitutive element of modernity' (Greenfeld, 1992, p. 18). Based on an impressive array of literary evidence, she again sought to refute the claims of modernism, arguing that not only was national sentiment pre-modern among elites, but that such loyalties were also shared by the majority of the population of sixteenth-century England.

EXERCISE

This exercise will help to illustrate the type of evidence that Hastings, Greenfeld and others have based their arguments on. Read Anthology Documents 5.25, 'David Hume, "Of national characters"', and 5.26, 'William Shakespeare, *Henry V*'. The first is an extract from an essay by the Scottish philosopher David Hume and the second (providing some light relief) is a passage from Shakespeare's play *Henry V*. As you read the two extracts, think about the following question: What does each extract suggest to you about the nature of national identity in England at the time of writing? You may wish to underline words or phrases that seem particularly significant to you, or which give strong clues as to the views of the author on the subject. Once you have read and annotated both extracts carefully, jot down a few lines in answer to the above question. Note in particular *when* each extract dates from.

Spend about 30 minutes on this exercise.

SPECIMEN ANSWER

Taking the Hume extract first, this appears to show that the author is convinced that different 'peoples' or 'nations' can be identified in Europe. He has strong opinions on the characters of different national groups, too. National stereotypes are clearly not a modern phenomenon. Hume also appears to discuss national identity and government at the same time. In other words, he is not merely identifying a 'cultural' English nation, divorced from politics. As he notes, 'Where a number of men are united into one political body ... they must acquire a resemblance in their manners, and have a common or national character'. Of course, it is hard to determine the extent to which Hume's beliefs were shared by the bulk of the population. Nevertheless, this extract at least does appear to run counter to those theories which claim that nation states are purely modern and that thinking about national identity before the onset of industrialisation was restricted solely to the cultural sphere.

The passage from Shakespeare is perhaps slightly harder to interpret. The extract itself again appears to indicate that national sentiment can be found significantly before the modern period. It conveys the sense that people living in England would identify themselves so closely with their nation that they would be willing to sacrifice their lives to retain its integrity. The final exhortation 'Cry "God for Harry! England, and Saint George!"' neatly combines devotion to the monarch, love of country and the power of religion in a stirring call to arms. This is, of course, a drama – a fictional work. The use of works of literature by historians to provide 'evidence' about the past is not universally accepted. We cannot know with certainty whether Henry V and his troops spoke these words and responded accordingly (and, in fact, it is rather unlikely). However, we might argue that the very fact that Shakespeare chose to dramatise the events in this way indicates that *when he was writing* (in *c.*1599) this was a normal and accepted way to think about the nation. The extract thus again indicates that significantly prior to the onset of industrialisation, at least some residents of England believed a distinct English nation existed. This nation was not purely cultural but was also intrinsically linked to the English state.

It is interesting to note that Hume was writing in 1753. It was not until 1769 that James Watt filed his patent for a steam engine, arguably the start of the Industrial Revolution. Over the next century of British history there was rapid transition from an agricultural society to an industrial one, but Hume was writing in a mainly agricultural age, certainly before the onset of the 'modernity' that appears so significant to Gellner and others when considering the rise of national identity.

Hume was himself Scottish, and a major figure in the Scottish Enlightenment. The 1707 Act of Union had joined England and Scotland (formally creating the kingdom of Great Britain – see Figure 19.9), and musing on the question of whether Scotland and England would become integrated was a common theme of the Scottish Enlightenment.

The evidence provided by medievalists and early modernists has only slightly modified the prior consensus among many historians that nationalism and the rise of nation states were intrinsically linked to events in the nineteenth century. Everyone (even those contesting the modernity of national identity) agrees that there *was* a significant development of nation states and a concrete consolidation of national identity during the nineteenth century. It is really only the examples of England and France that appear to run counter to the ideas of 'classical modernism'. However, there has recently been another type of challenge to the modernists – one which is more subtle and compelling than those discussed above. One of the foremost historians of nationalism, Anthony D. Smith, gradually came to believe that nation states as we know them probably are modern, but that they are not really comprehensible without some investigation of their deeper roots, the ethnic communities or *ethnies* that preceded them. While initially an advocate of Gellner's ideas (and in fact one of Gellner's doctoral students), Smith gradually came to find the strict modernism of Gellner and others essentially unconvincing. He believed that those who stressed the modernity of nationalism systematically overlooked 'the persistence of ethnic ties and cultural sentiments in many parts of the world, and their continuing significance for large numbers of people' (Smith and Gellner, 1996, p. 361). In other words, if we are to account for such a significant historical development as the rise of nation states and national identity, we need to combine a focus on the mechanisms by which this occurred during the nineteenth century with a look backwards at the ethnic communities from which modern nations were formed. Only such a combined approach, Smith argues, can be convincing.

Smith's approach has been described by others (and more recently by himself, too) as 'ethno-symbolism' (Guibernau and Hutchinson, 2004, p. 1–8). Its basic

Figure 19.9 'Articles of the Union of the Parliaments being Presented to Queen Anne', 1706, from *Historic Acts of the Queens of England*, engraved by Valentine Green, 1786 after an original work by Johann Gerhard Huck. Private Collection. Photo: The Bridgeman Art Library. The articles stated that Scotland could contribute sixteen representative peers and forty-five members of the House of Commons in the united government, which was a meagre proportion. In return for a commitment to the succession of the house of Hanover to the British throne, Scotland received 'full freedom and intercourse of trade and navigation' and £398,085 10s (known as the 'Equivalent') for acceptance of a share of British debt

premise is that modern political national*isms* (the idea that coherent cultural groups should govern themselves) cannot be explained without reference to earlier ethnic ties and memories. Modern nations, for Smith, were formed from (and draw their emotive power from) prior ethnic communities. These ethnic communities are defined by Smith as:

> Named human populations with shared ancestry myths, histories and cultures, having an association with a specific territory and a sense of solidarity.
>
> (Smith, 1986, p. 32)

Ethno-symbolism does not claim that *all* nations are founded on earlier, ethnic communities – rather, that '*many* such nations have been and are based on these ties, including the first nations in the West – France, England, Castile, Holland, Sweden', and that nations such as France and England have acted as 'models and pioneers of the idea of the "nation" for others' (Smith and Gellner, 1996, p. 361). This analysis of the origins and genealogy of nations, especially in relation to the ties of ethnicity, has been the subject of most of Smith's work. Overall, however, his contention is that nations require some things that are intrinsically modern, such as a legal code of common rights, a unified economy, a compact territory and a single political culture. Yet, crucially, '"nation-building" is not simply a matter of establishing the appropriate institutions or generating a complex class structure around a communications infrastructure' (Smith, 1986, p. 206). To survive, a nation must operate on two levels – the socio-political and also the 'cultural-psychological', and it is in this regard that nationalism (as well as the nation) is dependent on the 'earlier motifs, visions and ideals' generated by ethnic communities (Smith, 1991, p. 69). Smith's 'ethno-symbolism' thus attempts to supplant prior monocausal explanations of the rise of nation states, and to transcend the 'are they modern or aren't they?' questions that beset much earlier work. While not compulsory at this point, if you wish you can read about Smith's ideas in a little more detail in chapter 8 of his 1998 book, *Nationalism and Modernism*, which is available on the course website.

As you might perhaps guess by now, however, not everyone agrees with Smith. Some historians have argued that Smith makes too much of the link between pre-modern ethnic groups and nations. Eric Hobsbawm, for example, has claimed that while some ethnic groups do eventually end up as nation states, the transformations involved are so complete that the significance of ethnicity must be minimal. It is therefore modernisation, rather than ethnicity, that is the important factor. Ernest Gellner, asking the question 'Do nations have navels?', similarly argued that because it is possible to find some examples of nations that are completely novel (he cites the Estonians here, who did not even have a collective name for themselves at the start of the nineteenth century), the argument about prior ethnic groups falls down. For Gellner, if even a small minority of nations can be proved to be the product of modernity, then in other cases where the nation *appears* to have deeper roots, this must be an illusion (Smith and Gellner, 1996).

It is always potentially confusing (and frustrating for history students) when historians disagree with each other to the extent to which they have over the issues of nationalism and national identity. The development of multiculturalism and greater ethnic diversity in western European nations during the last twenty years has further complicated the issue. Recent research has highlighted the contested nature of national identity, with some authors even questioning whether such a thing still exists. Stuart Hall, for example, has argued that the nation state is now 'beseiged' by larger communities wanting to absorb it from above and by the rediscovery of face-to-face communities challenging it from below (Hall, 1996, p. 345). Benedict Anderson, too, has identified what he refers to as 'the impending crisis of the hyphen', and believes that national groups will increasingly become uncoupled from the state forms to which they were shackled during the nineteenth and twentieth centuries (Balakrishnan, 1996, p. 8). If this topic interests you, can read a brief summary of recent writings on the nation state in the extract from my 2005 book, *Nationalism: History and Theory*, which is available on the course website. However, the important point to remember is that disagreements between historians are a natural part of the progress of the discipline of history. As students, you will want to weigh up the various arguments and come to your own conclusions as to which you find the most convincing. The conclusion to this unit will help you to draw together the various ideas discussed above.

CONCLUSION

We have seen that there is a lot of evidence that European populations formed significant new relationships with the states in which they resided, and that a new conception of citizenship was consolidated, in the century or so after the French Revolution. A number of new 'nation states' were formed, and patriotism and other expressions of national identity were significantly more widespread at the end of the century than at the start. However, we have also seen that there is a lot of debate about *why* this happened. There is also, of course, debate about precisely *when* this happened. As we have seen, historians such as Eugen Weber have argued that, even by the second half of the nineteenth century, the populations of some of Europe's oldest nation states (such as France) felt more allegiance to their region or even their town than they did to a far-away capital. Other historians have argued the inverse – that, in fact, recognisable national sentiment may have existed long before the industrial revolution and the advent of 'modern society'. Do not worry if you have found some of the ideas or concepts discussed in this unit a little hard to get to grips with initially. This is complex material and historiographical debate does take time to assimilate. The following exercise will help you to draw together your thoughts on the rise of nation states in Europe.

This exercise has three parts. First, I would like you simply to draw up a list (probably quite a long one) of all the factors you recall mentioned in the unit that have been cited by historians as influential in the evolution of nationalism and national identity. Second, I would like you to look down this list and attempt to group the factors under the following headings – 'Economic factors', 'Political factors', 'Cultural factors' and 'Social factors'. It will probably be best to write the factors out again in four columns. Some of your list items might well fit under more than one heading. Finally, I would like you to see if you can attach the names of some of the historians mentioned to some of the sets of factors you have listed. For example, you might write 'industrialisation' or 'Industrial Revolution' on your first list. This would then come under the heading of 'Economic factors' on your second list, and you might then attach the name of Ernest Gellner to that particular factor. It is unlikely from the reading you have done for the unit that you will be able to assign a historian's name to every variable. Have a brief glance at the specimen answer before you begin if you need further clarification.

Spend about 30 minutes on this exercise.

List 1

- industrialisation or Industrial Revolution
- invention of printing
- spread of newspapers
- influence of key individuals
- development of modern bureaucratic states
- armed conflict or wars
- memory of the past
- 1848 revolutions
- liberalism
- fiction/plays
- conscription/tax collecting
- building of war memorials
- development of railway networks
- rise of democracy
- German philosophy
- language(s)
- impact of the French Revolution
- decline of organised religion
- breakdown of empires
- popular revolutionary organisations
- *Zollverein* – economic unification
- national anthems and flags
- education
- urbanisation
- ethnic communities

List 2

Economic factors

- industrialisation or Industrial Revolution
- invention of printing
- development of railway networks
- *Zollverein* – economic unification
- urbanisation

Political factors

- influence of key individuals
- 1848 revolutions
- liberalism
- conscription/tax collecting
- armed conflict or wars
- rise of democracy
- impact of the French Revolution
- breakdown of empires
- popular revolutionary organisations

Cultural factors

- memory of the past
- fiction/plays
- building of war memorials
- German philosophy
- decline of organised religion
- national anthems and flags

Social factors

- spread of newspapers
- influence of key individuals
- development of modern bureaucratic states
- armed conflict or wars
- language(s)
- education
- ethnic communities

List 3

Economic factors

- industrialisation or Industrial Revolution – *Ernest Gellner*

- invention of printing – *Benedict Anderson*
- development of railway networks – *Eugen Weber/Eric Hobsbawm*
- *Zollverein* – economic unification
- urbanisation – *Eric Hobsbawm/Ernest Gellner*

Political factors

- influence of key individuals – *John Breuilly*
- 1848 revolutions
- liberalism
- conscription/tax collecting – *Eugen Weber*
- armed conflict or wars
- rise of democracy
- impact of the French Revolution
- breakdown of empires
- popular revolutionary organisations

Cultural factors

- memory of the past – *Anthony Smith*
- fiction/plays
- building of war memorials – *Eric Hobsbawm*
- German philosophy
- decline of organised religion – *Benedict Anderson*
- national anthems and flags – *Eric Hobsbawm*
- social factors
- spread of newspapers – *Benedict Anderson*
- influence of key individuals – *John Breuilly*
- development of modern bureaucratic states – *Eric Hobsbawm*
- language(s) – *Anthony Smith/Benedict Anderson*
- education – *Eugen Weber/Ernest Gellner*
- ethnic communities – *Anthony Smith*

DISCUSSION

It will be readily apparent from drawing up your lists that there is really very little that has *not* been cited by historians at some point as vital to the development of nation states and national identity. Which explanations or theories do you find the most convincing? There is no 'right' answer to this question. It is likely that some of you will favour explanations that focus on the political sphere and the actions of key individuals, while others will be more attracted to theories that offer more abstract structural insights.

It might be tempting to believe that, given the diversity of nation-state formation and the disagreements over the reasons why, no unified explanation will ever be possible. However, this is perhaps unduly pessimistic. The balance of research so far seems to suggest that nation states *are* intrinsically linked with the rise of modern industrial society (although this is not to say that the odd one might not have existed beforehand) *but* that they are inexplicable without a consideration of the deeper roots that make this type of attachment/ sentiment so compelling and enduring. This unit has argued that an insight into the topic of nationalism and a knowledge of the formation of nation states are essential to any understanding of Europe during the nineteenth century. It has also contended that monocausal historical explanations are unhelpful when considering a topic as broad as nation-state formation. It is likely that a broad range of variables need to be invoked when considering the rise of nation states during the nineteenth century. That said, as briefly touched on, there is no doubt that one significant factor in the rise of national sentiment during the nineteenth century was the development of the historical profession itself. Historians were often the most vocal advocates of both existing and their role in this regard will be the subject of the following unit.

REFERENCES

Anderson, B. (1991) *Imagined Communities. Reflections on the Origin and Spread of Nationalism*, London, Verso.

Balakrishnan, G. (ed.) (1996) *Mapping the Nation*, London, Verso.

Baycroft, T. (1998) *Nationalism in Europe 1789–1945*, Cambridge, Cambridge University Press.

Breuilly, J. (1993) *Nationalism and the State*, Manchester, Manchester University Press.

Connor, W. (1990) 'When is a nation?', *Ethnic and Racial Studies*, vol. 13, no. 1, pp. 92–103.

Fulbrook (1993) *National Histories and European History*, London, UCL Press.

Gellner, E. (1983) *Nations and Nationalism*, New York, Cornell University Press.

Greenfeld, L. (1992) *Nationalism. Five Roads to Modernity*, Cambridge, Mass., Harvard University Press.

Guibernau, M. (1996) *Nationalisms: The Nation-State and Nationalism in the Twentieth Century*, Cambridge, Polity Press.

Guibernau, M. and Hutchinson, J. (2004) *History and National Destiny: Ethnosymbolism and its Critics*, Oxford, Blackwell.

Hall, S. (1996) 'Ethnicity: Identity and Difference' in Eley, G. and Suny, R.G. (eds), *Becoming National. A Reader*, Oxford, Oxford University Press, pp. 338–53

Hastings, A. (1997) *The Construction of Nationhood. Ethnicity, Religion and Nationalism*, Cambridge, Cambridge University Press.

Hobsbawm, E. (1990) *Nations and Nationalism since 1870. Programme, Myth, Reality*, Cambridge, Cambridge University Press.

Lawrence, P. (2004) *Nationalism. History and Theory*, Harlow, Pearson.

O'Leary, B. (1997) 'On the nature of nationalism: an appraisal of Ernest Gellner's writings on nationalism', *British Journal of Political Science*, vol. 27, pp.191–222.

Rath, P. (1964) 'The Carbonari: their origins, initiation rites, and aims', *The American Historical Review,* vol. 69, no. 2, January, pp. 353–70.

Seligman, M. and McLean, R. (2000) *Germany from Reich to Republic 1871–1918*, Basingstoke, Macmillan,

Silone, I. (1937) *The Living Thoughts of Mazzini*, London, Cassell.

Smith, A.D. (1986) *The Ethnic Origins of Nations*, London, Blackwell.

Smith, A.D. (1991) *National Identity*, London, Penguin.

Smith, A.D. and Gellner, E. (1996) 'The nation: real or imagined?: The Warwick debates on nationalism', *Nations and Nationalism*, vol. 2, no. 3, pp. 357–70.

Snyder, L.L. (1964) *The Dynamics of Nationalism*, New York, Van Nostrand.

Weber, E. (1977) *Peasants into Frenchmen. The Modernization of Rural France 1870–1914*, London, Chatto and Windus.

Paul Lawrence

INTRODUCTION

> Historians are to nationalism what poppy-growers ... are to heroin-
> addicts: we supply the essential raw material for the market.
>
> (Hobsbawm, 1990, p.3)

As you have seen in Unit 19, the nineteenth century witnessed a complex
series of social, economic and political changes that seem to have produced a
new type of relationship between many populations and the states in which
they lived. A number of new 'nation states' were formed and the sentiment of
'national identity' (feeling an integral part of, and a duty of loyalty to, a
particular 'nation') spread widely in Europe. As you now know, a variety of
different explanations have subsequently been posited to account for these
developments. Much of this debate has been based on a tension between those
who believe that *ideas* (whether political, cultural or philosophical) are the
prime source of historical change, and those who highlight more concrete,
structural factors (such as the economic and technological developments
associated with 'modernisation'). In fact, as we have seen, it seems likely that
a range of factors came into play at the same time, and that no single
explanatory variable will ever be found. That said, this unit will aim to supply
a case study of one particular factor that was influential in the rise of national
sentiment during the nineteenth century – the rise of the historical profession.

It is probably fair to say that prior to the nineteenth century there was no
academic discipline of history writing as we understand it today. This is not to
say, of course, that there was no concern with the past *per se*. Works of history
were obviously written before the nineteenth century. The term first entered
general usage in English in 1531 and you have already encountered the work
of two seventeenth-century historians in Unit 10. However, before the early
part of the nineteenth century there were no historians working in universities
and no historical journals. In other words, there was no historical profession as
we have today. The French historian Jules Michelet, for example, initially
taught philosophy. When he was appointed to teach history at the Collège
Sainte-Barbe in 1822, the subject had only recently been added to the
curriculum and was still viewed with suspicion by the government. More
significantly, before 1800 there was no real historical *methodology* as we
would now understand the term. Our current historical methodology –
involving trips to the archives to read primary sources, with the aim at least of
objectivity (the elimination of bias) – only developed gradually during the
nineteenth century. While pioneering historians such as the German Leopold
von Ranke argued that the use of primary sources was vital, and that the aim of
the historian should be to recount the past 'wie es eigentlich gewesen' ('as it
actually was'), many nineteenth-century historians fell far short of his ideals.

As the historical profession developed, it became closely linked with the growth of nation states, and historians often emerged as the most vocal spokesmen for national projects.

EXERCISE

As a brief introduction to this topic, read Anthology Documents 5.27, 'Introduction to Macaulay's *History of England*', and 5.28, 'Guizot's *History of Civilization in Europe*'. These are short extracts from the works of two well-known nineteenth-century historians – Thomas Macaulay and François Guizot. As you read, consider the following questions. How would you characterise the depictions of England and France implicit in the work of these two historians? What do you think the effect of reading this type of historical writing might be? How does this type of historical writing differ from some of the more modern works of history you have encountered during this course? There is no need to write out answers in full, but jot down a few notes in answer to each question as you read.

Spend about 30 minutes on this exercise.

SPECIMEN ANSWER

Clearly, both historians viewed their own nation state as more 'significant' than others. Macaulay's glowing account of England (of which more later) reads as a rather complacent account of success and progress, and certainly does not seem at all balanced. Guizot's depiction of France as the motor of civilisation in Europe also appears somewhat slanted. Indeed, these extracts appear almost ludicrously partisan to the reader of today. It seems that Macaulay and Guizot did not aim at the detached objectivity that is usually the goal of the modern historian, but rather sought in their writing to stimulate national pride in their readers.

DISCUSSION

Before we condemn such writings out of hand, however, two points need to be considered. First, it must be remembered that these authors were writing at a time when the practical ramifications of the idea of nationalism were still unfurling. The political and social turmoil of Europe during the nineteenth century was considerable, and both authors were involved in the political life of their countries (see Figure 20.1). In the period to 1870, as you know, many of the nation states that exist today were still only in the process of formation. It is thus important to bear in mind that the new 'national' histories of the nineteenth century were written in a highly charged political and social context.

Moreover, in addition to this broader context, the somewhat fledgling nature of the historical profession at this time must also be considered. Stefan Berger notes that, while 'the nineteenth century witnessed the increasing professionalisation of historical writing', it was also true that most nineteenth-century historians wrote *national* histories, and usually showed 'remarkable zeal in demonstrating the uniqueness of their particular nation-state' (Berger, Donovan and Passmore, 1999, p. 12). Macaulay and Guizot were by no means unique. Even historians not directly involved in nationalist or state-building endeavours (and many were) generally assumed without question that their nations 'had a unique right to sovereignty and political representation' (Suny, 2001, p. 346).

Figure 20.1 Eugène Lami, *Reception in Honour of Queen Victoria and Prince Albert at the Château d'Eu on 3 September 1843*, 1845, oil on canvas, .83 x 1.45 m. Châteaux de Versailles et de Trianon, Versailles. Photo: © RMN / © Gérard Blot. As well as a noted historian, François Guizot was a key government minister during the 1830s. In this picture, Queen Victoria is seated at the table. On the settee to the left of the picture, Louis-Philippe is in conversation with Prince Albert. Immediately in front of them, Guizot is talking to Lord Aberdeen. It was not uncommon for those writing works of national history to be intimately connected to the governments of the countries they wrote about

The Earl of Aberdeen (1784-1860), fourth Earl. George Hamilton Gordon. "took little part in politics, preferring farming & antiquarian" pursuits.
Foreign Secretary (1828-1830
                    & 1841)   "was instrumental in pulling relations with France back from the brink of war." Although the
                    ↓   guarantees he later received from Guizot over France's dynastic intentions in Spain later proved worthless."
                   poor.

Prime Minister (1852-55) of a coalition: Lord Russell : F.O
[Whigs themselves a coalition]   Palmerston : H.S.
                                        Gladstone : Chancellor

Foreign Secretary (+ 1841)
Palmerston 1830-1841

Thus, while the previous unit gave an insight into some of the key events of nation formation during the nineteenth century, and also considered some of the main explanations subsequently posed by present-day historians, the focus of this unit will be on how those living and writing *at the time* interpreted the rise of 'nation states'. The first section of this unit, 'Nineteenth-century historians and "the nation"', will give an outline of the development of the historical profession in France, Germany and Britain. It will show the ways in which history writing in general was linked to the rise of national sentiment. In the second section, 'Nineteenth-century "theories" of nationalism', we go on to consider some nineteenth-century writings specifically concerned with nationalism, and discuss how these were inevitably influenced by the 'national' histories being written at the time. The third section, 'Dissenting voices', however, will consider those who swam against this tide. While there was mass enthusiasm for 'nation building' and the spread of national sentiment during the nineteenth century, there were some dissenting voices. It is easy to overlook the fact that not everyone during the nineteenth century thought that nationalism was a good thing, and this section will consider the views of such authors, and also ask why they were ultimately marginal.

It will be apparent that the main subject matter of this unit is somewhat different from the others in this block. This unit is primarily concerned with *ideas* – their production, spread and significance. For historians, consideration of the place of 'ideas' in the past is important for two reasons. In the first place, it is easy to forget that there is much more to the study of lives past than the regurgitation of facts and figures, and the bland tracing of 'what happened'. Just as the often intangible currents of ideas can affect our lives today (think, for example, of the significance of the rise of environmentalism and the spread of the green movement), so a consideration of how people in the past *thought* about their societies is vital to a complete understanding of an era. More specifically, no full understanding of why nationalism became such an important force during the nineteenth century is possible without an appreciation of the role that history writing and remembrance of the past had in the process of building a nation state. It is also important, of course, to recognise that history writing is not (and has never been) value free. Historians write in a specific social and historical context, and their work (perhaps inevitably) reflects the ideas and social perspectives in vogue at their time of writing.

Before we get going, just a brief word about terminology. One term you will encounter quite a bit in this unit is 'historiography'. You have already come across a discussion of this in Unit 10, but a brief recap is perhaps appropriate. Put simply, historiography means 'the writing of history' or 'written history'. In other words, if we consider the 'historiography' of the French Revolution, we are considering all the works of history which deal with that topic. Likewise, if we talk about nineteenth-century British historiography, we are referring to the history books published in Britain during that century. Historiography is, if you like, the 'history of history writing'. As with the previous unit, the subject matter you will encounter here can be complex at times. For this reason, this unit is a little shorter than the others in the block, and has fewer exercises. So, take a deep breath, take your time and enter the world of nineteenth-century 'historiography'.

NINETEENTH-CENTURY HISTORIANS AND 'THE NATION'

In order to understand how people in the nineteenth century viewed the startling upsurge of national sentiment during their century, it is important first to consider the development of the historical profession. The way in which the academic profession of history was forming in different countries, and the emerging trends of historical writing thus introduced, have immense relevance to early debates on nationalism. Issues of identity were 'universal questions' for nineteenth-century European states, whether or not they underwent territorial upheaval, and in the main it was early historians who attempted to answer these questions (Jones, 2000, p. 43). Despite this, however, detached debate on the origins and spread of nationalism, and indeed even specific writings on the subject, were rare. Instead, as Stefan Berger notes, 'Almost every nation or would-be-nation had its historical nation-builders: historians who set out, often in multi-volume works, to narrate the history of their particular nation' (Berger, 2002, p. 2).

Very different traditions of thinking about nations and nationalism can be unearthed from within the varied national histories written across Europe during the latter half of the nineteenth century. This section of the unit will first consider the rise of the historical profession generally, and will then consider the links between history writing and national identity by examining the writings of three different historians – Heinrich von Treitschke, Jules Michelet and Thomas Babington Macaulay.

Modern academic history began to take shape at the beginning of the nineteenth century, with the first university chairs in history being created in Berlin in 1810 and Paris in 1812. Within a decade, historical societies had been created to collect and publish historical documents, and historians had founded their own professional journals (Iggers, 1997). There were, of course, both historians and history writing before this time, but professional, academic history, with its emphasis on primary sources and aspirations to a scientific methodology, was a nineteenth-century invention. Central to the early practice of professional history during the nineteenth century was the development of the 'historicist' approach in German universities, and its subsequent exportation throughout Europe. Take care not to confuse the term 'historicist' with 'historiography' (which was defined in the introduction). The essence of the historicist stance was that a fundamental difference existed between the phenomena of the natural world and the events of human history. Whereas previously it had been common to think about human existence in terms of 'natural law' – explicable by philosophical and religious investigation – historicists proposed a new way of understanding the rich diversity of man's historical experience. It was argued by early nineteenth-century historicists that there were no intrinsic *laws* of human nature, as in other spheres of the natural world, and that history, therefore, was the only guide to understanding things human.

This intellectual development served both to bolster the standing of the historical profession and to make the nation a legitimate object of enquiry for historians. However, although the unfolding of nations and nationalism henceforth needed to be researched and described, for the first generation of historicists this duty did not necessarily conflict with the notion of a divine plan for humanity. The pioneering German historian Leopold von Ranke was certainly the foremost early exponent of historicism, and indeed 'ultimately became the model for professionalized historical scholarship in the nineteenth century' (Iggers, 1997, p. 26). Appointed to a chair at the University of Berlin in 1825, Ranke aimed to turn history into an exact science, through the methodical evaluation and use of primary sources, and by the strict avoidance of value judgements. And yet, although history, for Ranke, had replaced philosophy as the 'science' that offered insights into the human condition, he retained a belief in a divine plan for humanity. For him, 'existing political states, insofar as they were results of historical growth, were "moral energies" or "thoughts of God"' (Iggers, 1997, p. 25). While aiming to reveal history 'wie es eigentlich gewesen' ('as it actually was'), for Ranke this primarily meant revealing the evolution of the existing order of things as God had willed it.

Thus the adoption of historicism did not imply 'objectivity' as we might now understand the term. While not all professional German historians (particularly later in the century) agreed with Ranke's belief that what had developed historically was sanctioned by God's will, many certainly shared his focus on the state as an almost mythical entity. This is perhaps unsurprising considering the close links between the German state and the historical profession. In nineteenth-century Germany (and, indeed, elsewhere) the state wielded considerable influence when it came to the appointment and promotion of historians at universities and research institutes. Freedom to criticise the state was not widespread during the early nineteenth century, and governments often had a clear idea of which histories and historians they wanted to promote. Certainly, foreign visitors such as the English historian John Seeley (normally extremely Germanophile) found it 'positively alarming' that German academics had 'in a certain degree the character of government officials' (Wormell, 1980, p. 67).

There is some dispute over this issue. It is possible that his status as a civil servant actually gave the university professor a high degree of protection against political pressure. It has also been argued that the state acted more as a 'facilitator' of money and status than as an outright sponsor, and that historians certainly liked to think of themselves as independent. However, as Bismarck used Prussia to transform Germany into a nation state, historians emerged as among the most vocal advocates for the project (see Figure 20.2). They considered themselves part of the *Bildungsbürgertum* – the educated and cultured bourgeoisie – and were clearly favoured by the system. As

Figure 20.2 G.Hyon, *An Episode in the Franco-Prussian War*, oil on canvas, 92.4 x 119.4 cm. Art Gallery and Museum, Kelvingrove. Photo: Glasgow City Council (Museums). In 1870, Emperor Napoleon III was manoeuvred into war with Prussia. On 2 September, at the head of his troops, he suffered a disastrous defeat at Sedan. The Prussian troops then laid siege to Paris, bombarding the city with canons for over four months. In January 1871, the interim French government was forced to sign a humiliating armistice with the new German empire. Historians such as Treitschke in Germany and Lavisse in France were strongly influenced by the war, and often framed their work accordingly

McClelland notes, 'those ... who found it possible to support the Imperial government in every twist and turn of its policy, were rewarded with posts and honors, which caused considerable adverse comment among less committed (but better qualified) scholars' (McClelland, 1971, p. 162).

The example of the historian Heinrich von Treitschke, whose contemporary influence was enormous, is instructive here. Treitschke's name is closely associated with his unswerving support for the national idea. You will recall the circumstances of German unification from Unit 19. Following unification in 1871, Treitschke held a seat as a National Liberal in the Reichstag, and 'observed with increasing apprehension the decline of the patriotic movement' (Winzen, 1981, p. 158). It was in this context that he began work on his *Deutsche Geschichte im neunzehnten Jahrhundert* (*German History in the Nineteenth Century*), published in a series of volumes between 1879 and 1894. In his own words, his express aim was not just to describe 'merely the context of the events', but also to arouse in the hearts of his readers 'what many of our fellow countrymen have lost today due to the unrest and discontent of the time, namely the pleasure of living in the Fatherland' (quoted in Winzen, 1981, p. 155).

Full of vitriol for the British, whom he described as 'dreadful hypocrites' with an empire based on an 'abundance of sins and outrages', the work was extremely well received in Germany. All leading figures, and many well-educated people, read it. Indeed, Chancellor Bernhard von Bülow noted that Treitschke's *German History* 'became the basis of my political way of thinking and feeling', and it reputedly prompted Alfred von Tirpitz's lifelong mistrust of Britain. In most of Treitschke's other works his primary concern (following Ranke) was with the state as the proper, primary focus of personal loyalty. However, his desire to justify German unification and expansion was always clear.

The idea that force (on the part of the state) was vital in national struggles was another theme running through his work. As he noted in *Die Politik* (*Politics*):

> War is political science *par excellence*. Over and over again has it been proved that it is only in war that a people becomes in very deed a people. It is only in the common performance of heroic deeds for the sake of the Fatherland that a nation becomes truly and spiritually united
>
> (Quoted in Davis, 1914, p. 150)

Thus history, for Treitschke, unfolded as a 'great process of attrition'. Through armed struggle between different nations, the 'power of the will' of successful nations was strengthened. Displaying again his belief in the primacy of the state, he noted that it was obvious that 'nothing is to be gained from barren talk about a right of nationality' (quoted in Davis, 1914, p. 188). While it was natural that nationalities would wish to make themselves politically independent, the key point to note was that 'every state must have the right to merge into one the nationalities contained within itself' (quoted in Davis,

1914, p. 188). If you think back to the attempts to incorporate Poles into the new German empire after unification, the political significance of such writings will become apparent. Of course, the response of minority nationalities to the threat of assimilation was often to write histories of their own, thereby staking their own claim to legitimacy.

Treitschke's historical works were thus typical of many texts produced at the time. His ideas were a product of his pre-existing political views, and the politically charged context in which he was writing. His focus on the significance of the state in the process of nation-state formation was typical of German historians and, above all, he sought to provide a historical *justification* for German unification and expansion. Similar concerns can also be discerned in the work of numerous other German historians. Much history writing in Germany prior to the First World War was redolent with the themes of national pride and national 'exceptionalism'. In this, of course, German historiography was not alone. Although not necessarily seeking to promote or justify territorial change at the time, it is easily possible to locate analogous examples in French and English historiography, and it is to these examples that we turn next.

In France, the historical profession was also developing rapidly during the nineteenth century. More works of history (as a percentage of total academic output) would be published during the long nineteenth century (to 1914) than during either the eighteenth or the twentieth centuries (Boer, 1998, p. 8). Certainly it was during the nineteenth century that history writing acquired an unprecedented status in France. Moreover, as was the case with Germany, a clear historiographical tradition eulogising the specificity of French nationalism developed, but it reached very different conclusions. Rather than politics and the power of the state, it was the French Revolution and the role of 'the people' that often formed the basis for the claims of French 'exceptionalism' in works of history.

A case in point is the historian Jules Michelet, erstwhile head of the Archives Nationales and appointed to a chair at the Collège de France in 1838. In his massive and popular *Histoire de France* (*History of France*), the first volume of which was published in 1833 and the seventeenth not until 1876, Michelet played down the role of great men (and 'the state') in the historical process and located the driving force of history in society at large. Eventually, Michelet came to see the French Revolution as the moment when nations (and France in particular) came into the final stage of self-consciousness, noting that the revolutionary leaders 'are usually but wrongfully considered as the sole actors. The fact is that they received rather than communicated the impulse. The chief actor is the people' (Michelet, 1967 [1844–47], p. x). The French Revolution has often been seen by subsequent historians as the birth of the modern idea of nationalism (the notion that a defined 'people' should have the right to govern itself), and Michelet was certainly one of the first to invest the Revolution with this level of significance.

EXERCISE

Now read Anthology Document 5.29, 'Michelet, *History of the French Revolution*'. This is an extract from Jules Michelet's *Histoire de la Revolution française*, published in 1848. As you read this extract, consider the following (quite difficult) questions: To what does Michelet attribute the birth of the French nation? And, how would you characterise the way in which Michelet writes about these events? In other words, what types of terms and expressions give you clues to Michelet's personal views on the matter? You might find it helpful as you work to underline or annotate any particularly telling phrases.

Spend about 30 minutes on this exercise.

SPECIMEN ANSWER

Michelet sees the French Revolution itself as the event through which the modern French nation was formed. For him, it was during this period that 'a whole nation, free from all party distinction ... marched as one beneath the flag of brotherly love'. His description of the course of the Revolution is couched in almost religious phraseology. He refers, for example, to 'that holy period' and 'the sacred days of the world'. He is clearly immensely proud of the fact that it was in France, his own nation, that this seminal event occurred.

DISCUSSION

Michelet conveniently ignores the virtual civil war that raged after the Revolution, and the slaughter of thousands of royalist supporters in the Vendée. As Gordon Wright has noted in his Introduction to Michelet's *History of the French Revolution*, Michelet's 'glowing patriotism' and his 'intense sense of Frenchness', combined with a strong current of universalism, meant that he came to view modern France as 'the brilliant culmination of universal history' (in Michelet, 1967 [1844–47], p. xi). As Michelet recalled in retrospect, 'I arrived both through logic and through history at the same conclusion: that my glorious motherland is henceforth the pilot of the vessel of humanity' (Michelet, 1967 [1844–47], p. xi). He believed that these views were justifiable because France had built its identity on the principles of liberty, equality and fraternity (see Figure 20.3). These were clearly 'universal values par excellence', and hence France's laws were 'only those of reason itself' (Todorov, 1993, p. 210). Clearly, like Treitschke, Michelet did not aim at objectivity. Rather, his history writing was coloured by national pride and full of political purpose. While the popularity of Michelet's work waned sharply after his death, it was very well received during his lifetime, and inspired in many significant public figures both patriotism and a belief in the unique mission of France to disseminate the values of the Revolution abroad.

Like Treitschke, Michelet showed little awareness of the problematic nature of the concepts about which he wrote but, interestingly, he came to an inverse view of the proper relationship between the state and the people (the nation). He concluded that legitimacy and the right to act lay with the people rather than with the state, continuing an intellectual tradition begun by Rousseau which viewed French nationalism as intrinsically liberal and inclusive. Analogous themes can also be discerned in the work of many other French historians. Ernest Lavisse, for example, was one of the most prominent French *belle epoque* historians. In 1888, Lavisse was appointed to the chair of modern history at the Sorbonne, a post that he was to hold for over thirty years. He was the editor of three monumental historical series, including the twenty-

Figure 20.3 Eugène Delacroix, *The 28th July 1830: Liberty Leading the People*, 1830, oil on canvas, 260 x 325 cm. Musée du Louvre, Paris. Photo: © RMN / © Hervé Lewandowski. This painting, though allegorical, was based on a contemporary event in 1830: a fierce, three-day uprising in the streets of Paris during which a republican mob forced the abdication of Charles X. Much of the street fighting took place near Delacroix's studio. Delacroix is said to have known all three of the main figures personally, particularly the boy, who killed a royal soldier before being badly wounded himself. Calling to mind the Revolution of 1789, it is often considered the painted equivalent of the French national anthem, 'La Marseillaise', and certainly showed that French pride in the revolutionary actions of 'the people' was not confined to historians alone

seven volume *L'Histoire de la France* (1900–11). His devotion to the 'idea' of France was also clear in his work. As he himself noted in the late 1880s:

> I know well that if I were to remove from myself certain feelings and certain ideas, the love of native soil, the long memory of ancestors, the joy of finding my soul in their thoughts and their actions, in their history and in their legends; if I were no longer to feel myself part of a whole of which the origin is lost in a haze and of which the future is uncertain; if I were no longer to thrill to the sound of a national anthem; ... if I were to forget our national sorrows, truly I would no longer be that which I am and that which I would be in this world. I would lose the main reason for living
>
> (Quoted in Nora, 1997, p. 322)

history as a means of 'glorifying' their state, their nation'.

Far from the objectivity we might expect from a historian, it is clear that, 'for Lavisse, France's "national teacher", history was a patriotic mission' (Boer, 1998, p. 289).

Thus a number of points can be drawn from the examples of Michelet and Lavisse. First, they both displayed a clear historical emphasis on 'the role of the people' and the importance of the Revolution in the delineation of French national identity. Second, while French historians were perhaps not as directly connected to the state apparatus as their German counterparts, both still advanced enthusiastic, if not partisan, depictions of their respective nations and were strongly influenced by their contemporary contexts. In the case of Lavisse, for example, it might be argued that his history of France is inseparable from the political and social context in which he was writing. The Franco-Prussian War of 1870/1, and the subsequent loss of Alsace-Lorraine, had forced a profound reorientation of French thought towards Germany. Having lost the war, and hence lost the ability to take pride in France as it was then, there was a concomitant redefinition of the French nation in terms of *history*, as opposed to other variables. History writing, for Lavisse, was a form of patriotic service. Thus in France, too, historiography hampered rather than facilitated critical analysis of the issues of nations and nationalism.

You will perhaps not be too surprised to learn that similar trends were developing in Britain, too, where the development of the nation was 'the principal inquiry of Victorian historians' (Jones, 2000, p. 52). Constitutional history was an important intellectual tradition that informed reflection on nationhood in nineteenth-century England. In contrast to the emphasis on the defining role of the state in Germany, and the impact of the Revolution and the 'will of the people' in France, English historians commonly placed an emphasis on parliamentary democracy at the centre of their accounts of English history and the development of English nationhood. Thomas Babington Macaulay's *History of England from the Accession of James II*, published in five volumes between 1848 and 1859, was one of the most acclaimed and popular English history books ever, selling over 140,000 sets. Macaulay traced the development of a libertarian parliamentary tradition, reaching back to the Magna Carta, and culminating in the Glorious Revolution of 1688.

Macaulay's *History* was a clear example of what came later to be known as a 'Whig interpretation' of English history (Butterfield, 1931). Members of a successful and powerful class, historians such as Macaulay commonly wrote complacent accounts of progress and success, which saw the whole of English history as leading inevitably to the present, ideal society (see Figure 20.4). Macaulay himself wrote that 'the history of England is emphatically the history of progress', and it is possible to see behind this assurance in progress the self-confidence of a reality that gave cause for political optimism. However, we must not forget that 'Whig' history could also serve reactionary purposes. Writing of this type helped to hold off parliamentary reform in England, on the grounds that the working classes were not yet ready for democracy but would be in the future (given the right sort of education).

Hence English historiography 'continued to serve political purposes, even if more covertly than in other European countries' (Berger, Donovan and Passmore, 1999, p. 38). Indeed, many of the great liberal historians of the nineteenth century made no secret of the direct political intentions of their work. Just as Ranke had noted that 'history ... prepares the way for a healthy policy' (quoted in Berger, 1997, p. 27), so the English historian John Seeley penned the maxim 'History without political science has no fruit; Political science without history has no root' (quoted in Wormell, 1980, p. 111). By this he meant that history should provide the backbone of sound policy making. Thus, even by the close of the century, general historiography in Britain, too, was deeply imbued with the paradigm of national exceptionalism and characterised by what would today be considered a lack of analytical impartiality.

EXERCISE

From the reading you have already done in this unit so far I would like you to write a short (one paragraph) answer to each of the following questions.

1   How would you characterise the relationship between historians and the state in the nineteenth century?

2   In what ways was the writing of history bound up with the rise of nationalist sentiment during the nineteenth century?

When writing your answers, it may be helpful to include/focus on some quotations from the extracts of nineteenth-century historical works that have been discussed in the unit so far. You may well want to look back through the unit in order to do this.

Spend about 30 minutes on this exercise.

SPECIMEN ANSWER

1   Professional, academic history writing is a nineteenth-century development. Various histories were, of course, written before this period but the *methodology* of history as we would recognise it today (including the use of primary sources) and also the very *aim* of modern history writing (the objective recreation of the past) were novel in the early nineteenth century. As such, the notion of historians as impartial, apolitical observers of the past was not as entrenched then as, arguably, it is now. Historians were often closely linked to the states in

Figure 20.4 Bristol riots. The Third Dragoon Guards attack rioters in Bristol, following public anger over the defeat of the Reform Bill by the House of Lords. Photo: Getty Images. Until the Reform Bill, the House of Commons had been elected in almost completely non-democratic ways. The 1832 Bill did not create a democracy, but it did enfranchise the British middle class. Lord Macaulay, a historian and Whig politician, was an active supporter of reform of the British parliament. His enthusiasm for and pride in British parliamentary democracy was readily apparent in his historical writing

which they lived. In Germany, in particular, but also in France and England, a two-way relationship existed between historians and governments. In Germany, for example, the state could create university chairs, vet appointments, apportion funding and give or withhold permission to publish. In return, on the side of historians, many were actively involved in politics and sought to use their writing to bolster support for the existing state apparatus. Men of ideas were often, of course, linked to the state in less formal ways, too. Being usually the same class as those who served in government, historians were likely to have very similar views of the state of the nation to those in the 'establishment'.

2   We have seen that historians could often be explicitly (and unashamedly) partisan in their work. For example, it was Treitschke's avowed intent to arouse in the hearts of his readers the 'pleasure of living in the Fatherland'. Rather than strive for the objectivity aimed at by the historical profession today (in theory, at least) nineteenth-century historians often wrote histories that set out to glorify their own particular nation state, actively selecting from the past to produce a version of history which served the twin aims of supporting the existing state structure and fostering national pride. Identifiably different historiographical traditions did emerge. In France, for example, the Revolution was seen as the defining moment in the development of the modern French nation. However, most national histories (of which many were written during the period) sought to glorify the nation state of the writer above all others.

This general discussion of nineteenth-century historiography has, of necessity, been rather short and selective. However, even this brief foray should have shown that it was not only 'new or immature nations' that sought 'to legitimize innovation by inventing a tradition' (Melman, 1991, p. 575). In England and France (as well as Germany) early professional historians customarily wrote without any real critical or analytical engagement with the concepts of nations and nationalism. Nations were often viewed as given, unified entities, and nationalism as an inevitable, or at least unproblematic, development. Historians often wrote with the explicit aim of fostering national pride. Moreover, nineteenth-century academic history was often written with implicit (and sometimes explicit) political aims, was strongly affected by international events, and was certainly mired within conceptions of national exceptionalism and distinctive national characteristics. Not all historians, of course, were unaware of (or chose to ignore) the complexities of their profession. Some writers did attempt to think more dispassionately about nationalism during the nineteenth century but, as we will see, found it difficult, if not impossible, to break free from the specific, *national* intellectual traditions within which they found themselves writing.

NINETEENTH-CENTURY 'THEORIES' OF NATIONALISM

As we have seen, modern historical writing was still in its infancy during the nineteenth century. Numerous 'national' histories were being written, often in response to ongoing political and social change, and it is easy to discern in these works an explicit desire on the part of the historians writing them to stimulate national pride and social cohesion. Objectivity, as we would now understand the term, was not a prime concern for many nineteenth-century historians. However, continuing with the theme of how those living in the nineteenth century thought about nations and nationalism, this section of the unit will consider the work of some nineteenth-century writers and thinkers who did attempt to write more dispassionately about nations and nationalism. Yet it will conclude that even those writing about nationalism and nation states in the abstract (in other words, not in relation to any particular country) were rarely what we might call 'objective', and were largely unable to break free from the nationalist perspectives outlined in the previous section of the unit.

It is clear with hindsight that most early 'theorists' of nationalism were strongly influenced by the developing national historiographical traditions within which they worked. The ideas of the French theologian Ernest Renan, for example, clearly reflect the persistent French emphasis on the defining role of the Revolution and its putative expression of the 'political will of the people'. Likewise, the British philosopher and political thinker John Stuart Mill was writing in a tradition that revered the role of representative government, and this is clearly echoed in his views on what constitutes a nationality. The pioneering German sociologist Max Weber never wrote the major work on nationalism he intended, but the comments that he did make on the subject reflected a tradition of national pride and a focus on the role of the state (as might be expected from an admirer of Treitschke). Thus, even those who professed to be writing 'scientifically' and 'objectively' about nations and nationalism appear to us today as rather biased, and often formulated their theories (subconsciously or otherwise) to shed a favourable light on their own nation.

Let us consider first one of the early 'theorists' of nationalism – Ernest Renan, born in France in 1823. You will recall that you have already encountered Renan in Unit 19. Renan primarily worked in another field, that of theology and ecclesiastical history, but perhaps his most enduring work began life as a lecture given at the Sorbonne on 11 March 1882 – *Qu'est-ce qu'une nation?* (*What is a Nation?*) (part of which is reproduced as Anthology Document 5.21). Reprinted countless times, this essay has become a classic text and an essential point of reference for much subsequent writing on the subject.

Renan's essay aspired to think more dispassionately about the issue. As he wrote in his preamble, he wished his analysis to be 'really a kind of vivisection', noting that 'we shall proceed coldly and with the utmost impartiality'. In fact, this was far from the case. Written in the wake of the Franco-Prussian War of 1870/1, in the light of ongoing territorial disputes over the annexation of Alsace and Lorraine, *What is a Nation?* was also, in part, a direct response and challenge to the work of Treitschke and his historical justifications of national expansion.

Renan's initial premise was that modern nations were 'something relatively new in our history' (Renan, 1996 [1882], p. 13). Since the break-up of the Roman empire in Europe, the developmental paths of different states had been marked primarily by the fusion of their diverse populations. France, for example, had only ever contained a minority of Francs. The modern nation was thus for Renan the result of a series of 'convergences' of different populations. This process could take place by dynastic ambition (as in the case of France), by the mutual agreement of provinces (as in the case of Switzerland), or by the action of a 'general will' (as in the cases of Italy and Germany). However, digging below the surface, Renan was also concerned to enquire as to how, or rather, on what basis, this process occurred. Let us now spend some time considering Renan's ideas in a little more detail.

EXERCISE

Now read the whole of Anthology Document 5.21 – an extract from Ernest Renan's *Qu'est-ce qu'une nation? (What is a Nation?)*, which was published in 1882. You have already used a short part of this in Unit 19. As you read the whole extract, think about the following questions.

1   What are the most important factors, for Renan, in the formation of a 'nation'?

2   How convincing do you find Renan's arguments? There is, of course, no single 'correct' answer to this question – the specimen answer gives just one possible view. However, you might like to consider your own sense of national identity, and think about how well Renan's analysis accords with your own experience.

One brief preliminary point to note is that Renan uses the word 'race' in a slightly different way from us. It was common during the nineteenth century to use the term to refer to any group of people sharing common biological descent. There is no necessary connotation of colour. Hence, the Italians could quite easily be described as a 'race'.

Spend about 30 minutes on this exercise.

SPECIMEN ANSWER

1   When writing about the rise of modern nation states, Renan considered the relative merits of *five* factors commonly cited as the basis of national sentiment: race, language, religion, community of interests, and geography. The study of 'race' he claimed to be of little utility. While probably important in ancient civilisations, modern nations were too racially mixed for this theory to hold any real truth. He contended that much the same objections could be advanced in relation to explanations of nationalism placing importance on language. This could certainly be a unifying force among populations, but to cite it as a 'fundamental determinant' was wrong, as the examples of Switzerland, the United Kingdom and the United States demonstrated. The idea of a 'community of interests', primarily economic, he dismissed cursorily, and notions of geography were equally quickly dealt with.

Having dispensed with these arguments, Renan then drew his famous conclusion (which we have already encountered in Unit 19) that, in fact, 'A nation is a soul, a spiritual principle.' For a nation to exist there are thus just two primary requirements. The first, historical, was the 'possession in common of a rich legacy of memories'. The second, primarily political, was 'the desire to live together, the will to perpetuate the value of the heritage that one has received in an undivided form'. He then gave his famous, voluntaristic definition of a nation as 'a daily plebiscite'. By this he meant that a nation only continued to exist if the members of the nation wanted it to. This sounds rather reminiscent of the 'will of the people' so popular in the national histories of Michelet and

Lavisse. Renan's image of the French nation as an ideal nation based on voluntary participation in a political experiment clearly drew heavily on representations of France already present within French historiography in general.

2   In many ways, Renan's analysis is quite perceptive. He captures quite well, with his notion of a 'daily plebiscite', the rather paradoxical concept that nations perhaps only exist because individuals believe they do. However, unlike modern works on nationalism, Renan's essay contains no footnotes, no quotations and no reference to primary sources. As a theologian, Renan's grasp of the detail of history was, perhaps patchy, and certainly he offers no really reliable evidence to back up his assertions.

DISCUSSION

Renan was one of the first writers on nationalism to aspire to an *analytical* methodology. However, his discussion is rooted in a deep-seated love of France, and imbued with a perception of his country as a bastion of liberty and a storehouse for 'universal values'. Demonstrating clearly the influence of the historical tradition in which he was writing, he noted in relation to the Revolution that 'it is to France's glory to have proclaimed, through the French Revolution, that a nation exists of itself', and asserted that 'we should not take it ill that others imitate us. The principle of nations is ours' (Renan, 1996 [1882], p. 23). Certainly, Renan's image of the French nation as an ideal nation based on voluntary participation in a political experiment drew heavily on representations of France already present within French historiography in general.

Michelet comes bf Renan.

Thus even Renan's bold attempt to think impartially about nations and nationalism was strongly influenced by both his own national pride, and the national histories of the type considered in the preceding section of this unit. In England, too, very weighty thinkers often struggled to think clearly about something that had shaped them so strongly (their own national identity), as the example of the noted philosopher and economist John Stuart Mill shows.

Born in 1806, Mill was a lifelong defender of individual freedom and human rights, and was one of the foremost British writers on social and political issues. It was in his *Considerations on Representative Government* (1861), arguing that representative (democratic) government was the most sensible compromise between the chaotic rule of the masses and the self-indulgence of the aristocratic few, that Mill made his most specific references to nationalism.

Mill took as his starting point the notion that there were two ways to think about the business of government. On the one hand, he noted that some people viewed the methods of government as nothing more than 'a practical art' (something created by logic and practical principles). Others, by contrast, invested government with much more significance, and saw it as 'organic growth', inherently rooted in 'the nature and life of people' (something which sprang from the very heart of a people's national identity). In other words, states were either nothing more than arbitrary ways of organising people, or were an expression of a deep national culture. Both views are obviously absurd when taken to extremes, but Mill inclined more towards the view that political institutions were in fact 'the work of men', and argued that there was 'a great quantity of mere sentimentality' connected with 'all that we are told about the necessity of an historical basis for institutions, of their being in harmony with the national usages and the like' (Mill, 1991 [1861], p. 18). The capacity for 'whole peoples' to learn new things should not be underestimated, he believed.

Thus, where Mill went on to write specifically about nationality, he gave a primarily *political* definition, claiming that:

> a portion of mankind may be said to constitute a nationality if they are united among themselves by common sympathies which do not exist between them and any others – which make them co-operate with each other more willingly than with other people, desire to be under the same government, and desire that it should be government by themselves, or a portion of themselves, exclusively.
>
> (Mill, 1991 [1861], p. 308)

There are certain similarities to Renan's arguments here. Such 'sympathies' could, for Mill, be generated by a variety of causes, but political antecedents (such as a national history and collective pride) produced the strongest sense of identity, although other factors, such as language and religion, could also serve in certain cases. He argued, unsurprisingly, that nationality should ideally be the primary determinant of governmental structures. However, he also went further to claim that free institutions (i.e. representative government) were simply not possible 'in a country made up of different nationalities' (Mill, 1991 [1861], p. 310). There would always be too much rivalry between different national factions, and the security against despotism provided by an army that identified entirely with the people would be absent under such circumstances. He concluded that 'for the preceding reasons, it is in general a necessary condition of free institutions that the boundaries of governments should coincide in the main with those of nationalities' (Mill, 1991 [1882], p. 313). He also believed that a nation was the largest unit to which an individual could feel a deep level of personal loyalty.

Mill made little objective enquiry into the nature of 'nations', which he treated as pre-existent and largely unproblematic, although he did concede that national identities could be subject to change over time. Moreover, his arguments were framed within prevailing notions of the 'biography of nations' and the notion of progressive civilisation. History, for Mill, was about 'progress' and hence if it were possible for one nationality to be absorbed into another, this should happen when 'it was originally an inferior and backward portion of the human race' (Mill, 1991 [1861], p. 314). Thus, taking the example of a Breton and a Basque in France, he concluded that it was more beneficial for individuals from these groups 'to be brought into the current of the ideas and feelings of a highly civilized and cultivated people', than to 'sulk on his own rocks, the half-savage relic of past times, revolving in his own little mental orbit, without participation or interest in the general movement of the world' (Mill, 1991 [1861], p. 314). Mill's views on nations were clearly based on the idea of a 'hierarchy' of nations, with established nation states such as England and France at the very top. Although, to be fair, in the case of Ireland (a topic which exercised him considerably during his time as a member of parliament), Mill felt that the main reason that Ireland had not gradually integrated into Great Britain was because the Irish had been 'atrociously governed' by the English.

If you are interested in Mill's ideas, an extract from his *Considerations on Representative Government* is included in your anthology as Anthology Document 5.30. However, it is clear that Mill was primarily concerned with finding a theoretical basis under which the doctrine of nationalism could serve the purposes of enhancing liberty (one of his main concerns). Thus, as with Renan, Mill's political background and aims (and his national background) were instrumental in shaping his thinking about nations and nationalism. It is also important to realise that most of these nineteenth-century writers were well aware of each other's work. Treitschke's *Die Freiheit*, for example, was written as a direct response to Mill's later work *On Liberty*. In turn, Renan's *Qu'est-ce qu'une nation?* was formulated partly in response to the strident nationalism of Treitschke's *Deutsche Geschichte im neunzehnten Jahrhundert* (*German History in the Nineteenth Century*). Thus, most nineteenth-century authors, even those who professed to think impartially about nations and nationalism, were still primarily writing from within an intellectual framework which assumed that both nations and nationalism were a good thing, and indeed often merely advocated one variant of nationalist doctrine over another. This was arguably the case even when the pioneering sociologist Max Weber is considered.

Weber, writing somewhat later than the authors discussed so far, was one of the founding fathers of modern academic sociology (along with Emile Durkheim). As with the historical profession, there had, of course, been sociological thinking before the late nineteenth century (one thinks, for example, of the work of Auguste Comte). It is common, however, to date the founding of modern sociology to between 1880 and 1920, when pioneering sociologists such as Weber and Durkheim sought a more scientific and detached understanding of human life. The first department of sociology was established at Chicago University in 1892, and social scientists often defined their approach in specific contrast to professional history, which they believed was too concerned with mere detail to have anything significant to say about human societies in general. However, even within the social sciences, there was still no *systematic* investigation into the phenomenon of nationalism. Direct comments on nation formation were primarily 'oddments', and neither Weber nor Durkheim (nor, for that matter, other prominent sociologists such as Georges Simmel) wrote much specifically on the issue of nationalism. Partly this may have been because, as was the case in the historical field at the time, any perceived necessity to 'theorise' the nation was 'obviated by the very prominence of the category of the nation' (James, 1996, p. 85). In other words, 'nations' were considered so self-evident that there appeared to be no need to explain them. This is still, arguably, the case today for many people. How often have you actually stopped to think about precisely *why* Europe is divided into separate nation states, and why this seems so significant to us?

Although he did not formulate specific theories of nationalism, the issues of national unity continually resurfaced in Weber's work. While his ideas were not that clearly defined before the First World War, he was later to advance the following incisive definition of the nation:

> If the concept of 'nation' can in any way be defined unambiguously, it certainly cannot be stated in terms of empirical qualities common to those who count as members of the nation. In the sense of those using the term at a given time, the concept undoubtedly means, above all, that one may exact from certain groups of men a specific sentiment of solidarity in the face of other groups. Thus, the concept belongs in the sphere of values.
>
> (James, 1996, p. 83)

A more extended version of Weber's ideas on the nation can be found in Anthology Document 5.31. However, even this brief definition captures well the elusive quality of national identity. This cannot, according to Weber, be defined in terms of specific qualities or traits that all members of a nation share. Rather, as Renan noted, national sentiment can best be summed up as a feeling of solidarity, or a belief that a debt of loyalty is owed to the abstract category of 'the nation'. What is important in a nation state is not that members are bound together by any specific criteria such as language or ethnicity, but rather that they *believe* they are. In other words, national identity is really a purely *subjective* phenomenon.

However, despite this insight, Weber's work was once again bound up with the political sphere, and with the (German) intellectual tradition in which he was writing. Weber was clearly influenced by the earlier work of Treitschke and, somewhat contradictorily given the innovative nature of his research, shared Treitschke's pride in the German nation (see Figure 20.5). Weber did not hesitate to draw on Darwinian metaphors when discussing the development of nations, and in the context of a discussion of Polish immigration referred to Germans as 'the more highly developed human type' (Guibernau, 1996, p. 37).

Moreover, Weber was a strong supporter of German participation in the First World War, noting that 'whatever the outcome, this war is great and wonderful' (Guibernau, 1996, p. 38). Despite his defence of a sociology that was value free, much of Weber's writing therefore consisted not of 'detached clinical analysis of social institutions' but of 'the defence of the values and public morality of a state-centred nationalist liberalism' (Harris, 1996, p. 350). In other words, he was a firm believer that national identity (and his own work) should serve a political purpose – a defence of the status quo in Germany.

Do not worry if you have found this second section of the unit a little tricky (the next section is more straightforward, and shorter). Getting to grips with intellectual history (how thinkers in the past viewed their own societies) is complex but worthwhile. It is only when we are armed with some knowledge of the *ideas* and *values* that were common in a particular period that can we

Figure 20.5 Jean-Joseph Weerts, *France!! Or Alsace and Lorraine Desperate*, oil on canvas, 170 x 230 cm. © Musée Lorrain, Nancy/photo: P. Mignot. When Renan wrote *What is a Nation?* in 1882, the recent loss of Alsace and Lorraine to Germany as a result of the Franco-Prussian War was clearly at the forefront of his mind. This loss continued to motivate artists, authors and thinkers until the First World War, when the territories were won back

fully understand it. A brief recap may be useful. The main points which I hope you have gleaned from the unit so far are:

1   Throughout the nineteenth century, it was common to assume the 'naturalness' of the nation state, and the inevitability of its development.

2   Most of those who considered the development of nation states (whether historians writing specifically about their own nation, or philosophers, political scientists or sociologists trying to write more generally) tended to emphasise the uniqueness and importance of their own particular nation state.

3   This meant that academic writings very often actively assisted in the formation/drawing together of nation states. Historians were among the worst culprits for this. The profession of history was relatively new to the nineteenth century, and historians often wrote histories specifically designed to stir national pride. Other thinkers, too, found it hard to step outside of their own backgrounds to write dispassionately about the topic.

We should not, however, judge the writers discussed so far too harshly. To put aside the assumptions of a lifetime and write objectively about a topic is probably impossible. Given that both modern history writing and sociological studies were new to the nineteenth century, and that (as discussed in the previous unit) the nation states we know today were only just forming, it is perhaps not surprising that those writing about national identity were more likely to be enthusiastic advocates than impartial observers. Interestingly, the very fact that so many nineteenth-century writers now appear 'biased' to us tells us quite a lot about just how entrenched and significant ideas about the 'naturalness' and 'desirability' of nationalism were at the time. However, while it is certainly true that most writers of the nineteenth century believed that both nations and nationalism were a good thing, and spent a good deal of time trumpeting their own version, there were some thinkers who swum against this tide. In the final section of this unit, we will consider some examples of writers who took a contrary view to the development of nation states.

DISSENTING VOICES

The names of two of the foremost thinkers who believed that nations and nationalism were generally not such a good thing will probably already be familiar to you. The ideas of Karl Marx and Friedrich Engels, the authors of *The Communist Manifesto* (which you have already encountered in Unit 18) and founders of the communist movement, were groundbreaking during the nineteenth century. At a time when, as we have seen, nationalism was perceived to be a primarily beneficial doctrine, and most historians were partisan supporters of their own nation states, Marx and Engels offered a radically different exploration of the role and desirability of both nations and nationalism. However, Marx and Engels (and later Marxist writers) by no means produced a comprehensive and convincing 'theory' of nationalism. There is no 'single theoretical (i.e. "scientific") and detailed study devoted to the national question' in their voluminous works (Fišera and Minnerup, 1980).

[handwritten margin note: "narrative histories"]

This gap has been called 'Marxism's great historical failure', but it might be claimed that Marx and Engels did still have a lot to say on the subject of nationalism, even though they did not provide any convincing answers (Nairn, 1975).

The earliest Marxist writings on nations and nationalism are contained within *The Communist Manifesto*, produced between November 1847 and January 1848 (a highly charged period both politically and socially, as you will recall from the previous units in this block – see Figure 20.6). The *Manifesto* was overwhelmingly the work of Marx, despite his generous attribution of co-authorship to Engels. Marx's primary concern in this famous tract was, of course, the delineation of his theory of 'historical materialism' (the idea that the form of human societies can be explained by economic and technological development), and the concomitant issue of class struggle as the motor force of history. For Marx, social classes were the proper objects of attention in the historical process. Local and national developments formed only a part, and an admittedly insignificant one, in the unfolding of historical change. The nation state, far from being a fundamental social category, was essentially, for Marx, simply a function and expression of *bourgeois* interests, and certainly secondary to the development of the economy. According to Marx, the need for constantly expanding markets had prompted the bourgeoisie to expand across the globe, and capitalism was thus increasingly rendering national sentiments irrelevant.

EXERCISE

I would like you to reread Anthology Document 5.16, '*The Communist Manifesto, 1848*'. Despite containing some startling new ideas and a revolutionary message (and being over 150 years old), you will notice that the *Manifesto* is quite easy to read and understand. This is because it was intended not as an in-depth, intellectual explanation of the capitalist system (as was another of Marx's works – *Das Kapital* (*Capital*)) but rather as a stirring call to arms. You will recall that 1848 was a period of revolutionary turmoil throughout much of Europe, and Marx and Engels were hoping to shape the course of this unrest. In the event, this did not occur, but the later impact of the *Manifesto* made it one of the most significant single documents of the nineteenth century. As you read the extract, consider simply the following question – what does Marx have to say about the future of nationalism and national sentiment? Once you have finished reading, draw together your ideas in a one or two paragraph answer to that question. The extract is reasonably long, to give you a full flavour of Marx's prose and ideas.

Spend about 40 minutes on this exercise.

SPECIMEN ANSWER

Unlike many commentators of the period, Marx clearly believed that national sentiment was not particularly important – either historically or at the time of writing. Rather, he claimed that 'class' and 'class struggle' were the really significant factors in the development of societies. At the time of writing, he saw Europe as divided more and more into two main classes – the bourgeoisie (who owned the 'means of production', such as factories and workshops) and the proletariat (who owned very little and sold their labour for wages). In order to prosper, the bourgeoisie needed continually both to oppress the proletariat and to seek out new markets for the goods they produced.

Figure 20.6 A revolution in Naples with barricades being set up in the Toledo just before the attack, 15 May 1848. Photo: Getty Images

As Marx put it – 'the bourgeoisie has through its exploitation of the world market given a cosmopolitan character to production and consumption in every country', leading to a situation in which 'in place of the old local and national seclusion and self-sufficiency, we have intercourse in every direction, universal inter-dependence of nations'. In other words, the oppression of poorly paid workers by industrialists had created a new social class, the proletariat, who now had more in common with each other across Europe than with the members of other classes of their own nation. In addition, the very search for new markets for the products of industry had also helped to break down national barriers and make everywhere the same.

Thus Marx seemed to have believed that nations and nationalism had no real future. Increasingly, workers would discover that they had more in common with each other than with those oppressing them within their own nation. Equally, the spread of the capitalist system would mean the end of national and local differences. Marx did point out that 'the struggle of the proletariat with the bourgeoisie is at first a national struggle. The proletariat of each country must, of course, first of all settle matters with its own bourgeoisie'.

DISCUSSION

Clearly, however, Marx and Engels overestimated the 'flattening force of internationalization' (James, 1996, p. 52). While a perceptive attempt to challenge the nationalist paradigm, this work was clearly a product of the prevailing *zeitgeist*. The mid nineteenth century was a period of massive social and political change throughout Europe. The disruptive impact of the twin forces of urbanisation and industrialisation was so sudden that it is perhaps easy to understand how it may have appeared to Marx and Engels as the defining feature of the period. Many governments were afraid that class might turn out to be more important than nation to the average man. *The Communist Manifesto* was written during a period of such rapid social change (and of such suffering on the part of many workers) that it is understandable that Marx and Engels felt that this would inevitably end in revolution.

While a socialist revolution did not, in the end, occur, the influence of Marxism on the course of European history is hard to underestimate. It is important, therefore, to remember that although the prevalent tide of ideas during nineteenth century was in favour of nationalism, there were counter-currents. As with any historical period, a broad mix of opinions, theories and ideas always existed. Certainly, it is possible to find other thinkers opposed to the doctrine of nationalism. One often-cited example is the Cambridge professor of modern history Lord Acton (see Figure 20.7), who was prompted by Mill's *Considerations on Representative Government* to investigate what he perceived to be theoretical flaws in Mill's argument. Acton's principal contribution to the debate on nationalism was the piece entitled 'Nationality', in his *Essays on Freedom and Power*, a section of which is reproduced in Anthology Document 5.32. Here, in common with other authors, he dated the origins of modern nationalism to the French Revolution which 'partly by its doctrines, partly by the indirect influence of events [...] taught the people to regard their wishes and wants as the supreme criterion of right' (Acton, 1956 [1862], p. 142). Unlike other authors, however, Acton did not necessarily regard this as a positive development, either at the time, or subsequently.

Figure 20.7 Photographer unknown, Lord Acton (John Emerich Edward Dalberg Acton, First Baron Acton) (1834–1902), professor of modern history at Cambridge. Photo: Getty Images

Acton believed that the example of the French Revolution and its aftermath demonstrated that the modern doctrine of nationalism (that every 'people' should govern their own affairs) was 'founded on the perpetual supremacy of the collective will', and that the unity of the nation was thus the overriding condition 'to which every other influence must defer'. Unlike most commentators, Acton advocated the presence of different nationalities within a single state, claiming it was 'as necessary a condition of civilised life as the combination of men in society' (Acton, 1956 [1862], p. 161). In a perceptive passage, worth quoting in full, he highlighted the contradictions inherent in the theory and practice of the doctrine of nationality, neatly predicting the practical ramifications of the assertion that every nation should govern itself:

> The greatest adversary of the rights of nationality is the modern theory of nationality. By making the State and the nation commensurate with each other in theory, it reduces practically to a subject condition all other nationalities that may be within the boundary. It cannot admit them to an equality with the ruling nation which constitutes the State, because the State would then cease to be national, which would be a contradiction of the principle of its existence. According, therefore, to the degree of humanity and civilization in that dominant body which claims all the rights of the community, the inferior races are exterminated, or reduced to servitude, or outlawed, or put in a condition of dependence.
>
> If we take the establishment of liberty for the realization of moral duties to be the end of civil society, we must conclude that those states are substantially the most perfect which, like the British and Austrian Empires, include various distinct nationalities without oppressing them. Those in which no mixture of races has occurred are imperfect; and those in which its effects have disappeared are decrepit.
>
> A State which is incompetent to satisfy different races condemns itself; a State which labours to neutralize, to absorb, or to expel them, destroys its own vitality; a State which does not include them is destitute of the chief basis of self-government. The theory of nationality, therefore, is a retrograde step in history ... Its course will be marked with material as well as moral ruin.
>
> (Acton, 1956, p. 168–9)

Acton's political inclinations could not really have been more different from those of Marx and Engels. Indeed, he believed the 'theory of socialism' to be both 'absurd' and 'criminal'. In addition, as a devout Catholic, he was firmly opposed to the atheism of the French Revolution, and this is clear in his writings on national development. However, his analysis of nationalism appears far-sighted today. This passage highlights clearly one of the contradictions inherent in nineteenth-century nationalism. While portrayed by many as a liberal and liberating doctrine (letting oppressed peoples govern themselves), the idea of nationalism did not actually work very neatly in practice. The boundaries of states very rarely coincided with the dispersal of groups considering themselves part of a nation. Think back to the complications discussed in Unit 19 in the case of Germany. Not only were there plenty of people who considered themselves German left living *outside* the German empire in 1871, but there were a large number who described themselves as Polish living *inside* the borders of Germany. This clearly did not make for harmonious relations, either internally or internationally.

While the views of both Acton and Marx (and the numerous other thinkers who opposed the new ideas of national sovereignty circulating during the nineteenth century) were influential, they ultimately fell by the wayside. The Europe in which we live today is overwhelmingly organised on 'national' lines. There are some signs that the European parliament, the European Court of Human Rights and other such supra-national organisations are beginning to erode the supremacy of national governments. However, it is clear that, for most people, their national identity is still one of the most fundamental components of their daily lives. A consideration of how this situation arose is vital to any understanding of Europe, both during the nineteenth century and today.

EXERCISE

To help you to draw together the various perspectives outlined in this Unit, I would like you to look back over the unit and considering the following question:

The nineteenth century was period when a number of new 'nation-states' were formed, and when national identity grew stronger in existing 'nation states'. How did historians and other commentators think and write about these processes at the time?

Spend about 30 minutes on this exercise.

EXERCISE

The modern historical profession was largely a nineteenth-century invention. It is probably no coincidence that the spread of the idea of nationalism (that every 'people' should govern themselves) and the writing of a large number of 'national' histories took place at the same time. Historians were often closely involved in the nation-building process. Historians commonly sought actively to stimulate national pride through their work, and certainly did not aim to write objectively or impartially.

Similarly, even those political scientists and sociologists who aimed to consider nationalism in the abstract, leaving aside particular examples, commonly failed to leave their own 'national' bias aside when writing. Renan's *What is a Nation?*, while purporting to offer a 'scientific' analysis of nations and nationalism, was in fact written partly in response to the strident German nationalism of historians such as Treitschke, and Renan's pride in the achievements of France certainly shaped the work.

DISCUSSION

The inability of many to think objectively about nationalism during the nineteenth century is not mentioned simply to criticise. After all, who knows what historians a century from now will make of the type of history currently being written? Rather, the importance of studying writings on nationalism during the nineteenth century lies in the insight it gives into European societies during the period. The enthusiasm that many writers displayed for their own nation states, and their desire to use their work to advance the cause of their own nations, shows that nationalism was one of the most significant political and social doctrines of the period. The German historian Johann Droysen, for example, was a member of the Frankfurt parliament and a leading proponent of the unification of Germany under his native Prussia. It is therefore probably no coincidence that his major work – *Geschichte der preussischen Politik* (*History of Prussian Politics*) portrayed German unification as the primary goal of Prussian politics. While there were some influential commentators (who now appear rather far sighted) who argued that nationalism was perhaps not as beneficial as most believed, this was a minority view during the period.

CONCLUSION

Overall, the precise significance of historical writing in the process of nation building is hard to gauge. This is something of a 'chicken and egg' situation. Did the ideas put forward by historians and other thinkers genuinely change popular attitudes, or did the writings of nineteenth-century historians mainly just reflect a process which was already under way? It is likely that both views contain an element of truth. Either way, the role of the historical profession in bolstering national sentiment is undeniable. Treitschke's call for Germany to take up the challenge of colonial expansion, for example, influenced many politicians. As he noted:

> today we distinctly see the peoples of Europe creating a mass aristocracy of the white race all over the world. He who does not take part in this gigantic competition is destined to cut a poor figure one day. Look how English speaking people figure in the world compared to their German speaking counterparts! It is therefore a vital question for the [German] nation to show colonial drive.
>
> (Quoted in Winzen, p. 1981, 160)

The period between about 1830 and 1890 was the high water mark of 'nationalist' histories of the type discussed in this unit. The First World War certainly tainted the doctrine of nationalism. However, even by the end of the nineteenth century, the term 'nationalism' was beginning to be associated less with the liberation of oppressed 'peoples' and more with the aggressive power politics of imperialism (see Figure 20.8). Indeed, the historian Peter Alter (among others) has argued that the nineteenth century witnessed the decline of early, liberal *Risorgimento* nationalism (typified by the unification of Italy) and its replacement by aggressive, expansionist *Integral* nationalism (Alter, 1994, p. 19–27). Alter argues that, while *Risorgimento* nationalism was characterised by 'the political fusion of large social groups, the formation of nations and the self-identification with the national state', the *Integral* nationalism of the later nineteenth century was typified by the slogan 'My country, right or wrong' and set one nation against all others. *Integral* nationalism is closely associated by Alter with 'imperialism' (the conquest of colonies overseas by the European powers), and this will be the subject of the next block.

Figure 20.8 Photographer unknown, British forces on parade in India, c.1900. Photo: Getty Images

REFERENCES

Acton, J.E.E.D., Lord (1956 [1862]) 'Nationality' in *Essays on Freedom and Power*, London, Thames & Hudson.

Alter, P. (1994) *Nationalism*, 2nd edn, London, Edward Arnold.

Berger, S. (1997) *The Search for Normality. National Identity and Historical Consciousness in Germany since 1800*, Oxford, Berghahn.

Berger, S. (2002) 'Representations of the past: the making, unmaking and remaking of national histories in western Europe after 1945', inaugural lecture held at the University of Glamorgan.

Berger, S., Donovan, M. and Passmore, K. (1999) *Writing National Histories. Western Europe since 1800*, London, Routledge.

Boer, P. den (1998) *History as a Profession. The Study of History in France, 1818–1914*, trans. A.J. Pomerans, Princeton, Princeton University Press.

Butterfield, H. (1931) *The Whig Interpretation of History*, London, G. Bell.

Davis, H.W.C. (1914) *The Political Thought of Heinrich von Treitschke*, London, Constable.

Fišera, V.C. and Minnerup, G. (1980) 'Marx, Engels and the national question' in Cahm, E. and Fišera, V.C. (eds) *Socialism and Nationalism*, vol. 3, Nottingham, Spokesman.

Guibernau, M. (1996) *Nationalisms. The Nation-State and Nationalism in the Twentieth Century*, Cambridge, Polity Press.

Harris, J. (1996) 'Platonism, positivism and progressivism: aspects of British sociological thought in the early twentieth century' in Biagini, E. (ed.) *Citizenship and Community. Liberals, Radicals and Collective Identities in the British Isles 1865–1931*, Cambridge, Cambridge University Press.

Hobsbawm, E. (1990) *Nations and Nationalism since 1870. Programme, Myth, Reality*, Cambridge: Cambridge University Press

Iggers, G. (1997) *Historiography in the Twentieth Century. From Scientific Objectivity to the Postmodern Challenge*, Hanover, Wesleyan University Press.

James, P. (1996) *Nation Formation. Towards a Theory of Abstract Community*, London, Sage.

Jones, H.S. (2000) *Victorian Political Thought*, London, Macmillan.

McClelland, C. (1971) *The German Historians and England*, Cambridge, Cambridge University Press.

Melman, B. (1991) 'Claiming the nation's past: the invention of an Anglo-Saxon tradition', *Journal of Contemporary History*, vol. 26, pp. 575–95.

Michelet, J. (1967 [1844–47]) *The History of the French Revolution* (ed. G. Wright), Chicago, University of Chicago Press.

Mill, J.S. (1991 [1861]) *Considerations on Representative Government*, New York, Prometheus.

Nairn, T. (1975) 'Marxism and the modern Janus', *New Left Review*, vol. 94, pp. 3–29.

Nora, P. (1997) 'L'Histoire de France de Lavisse' in Nora, P. (ed.) *Les Lieux de Mémoire. II. La national*, Paris, Gallimard.

Renan, E. (1996 [1882]) *Qu'est-ce qu'une Nation?/What is a Nation*, French/English edn, Ontario, Tapir Press.

Suny, R. (2001) 'History' in *Encyclopedia of Nationalism*, vol. 1, San Diego, Academic Press.

Todorov, T. (1993) *On Human Diversity. Nationalism, Racism and Exoticism in French Thought*, Cambridge, Mass., Harvard University Press.

Winzen, P. (1981) 'Treitschke's influence on the rise of imperialist and anti-British nationalism in Germany' in Kennedy, A. and Paul Nicholls, P. (eds) *Nationalist and Racialist Movements in Britain and Germany before 1914*, London, Macmillan.

Wormell, D. (1980) *Sir John Seeley and the Uses of History*, Cambridge, Cambridge University Press.

THE CENSUS AND THE STATE

Michael Drake

So far in this block we have been looking at the new kind of bureaucratic nation state that emerged during the nineteenth century. Unit 20 explored the role of historians in the development of 'nations' and 'states'. Here we will shift the focus to examine a tool of government that was increasingly employed by the new state. Moreover our examination will involve the development of IT skills that are of increasing relevance to contemporary historical scholarship.

Over the last two centuries the census has developed as a central feature of a state's infrastructure. How this came about is one aim of this section. The other is to show how, by using a computer, any individual can now analyse past censuses in ways that were beyond all the resources of the states that commissioned them.

CENSUSES

Counting the number of people in an area at a particular point in time can be traced back to biblical times. As the main aim was to find out the size of a population for tax and military purposes, the focus was on the adult male population. Modern censuses, however, are more than head-counts since they require a considerable amount of information about each individual, irrespective of age or gender. Such censuses emerged over the last 200 years, initially in the Nordic countries. They did not, however, become common in Europe until the second half of the nineteenth century. Just how common can be gauged by casting an eye over the top line of Table 1, where the names of the states conducting censuses in the 1870s and 1880s appear.

If you turn to the left hand column you will see what information all censuses should ideally seek. I say 'ideally' because this list of questions was drawn up by the heads of state statistical offices who, from 1853, met regularly to discuss such matters. They sought to produce a standard format that all states would follow but, as the body of the table shows, reality fell somewhat short of this ideal.

DISCUSSION

I suggest you now look at what each country required (indicated by a tick) and then consider the following questions.

1   What strikes you about the timing of the censuses?

2   What information was required by all the states and why?

3   More interestingly, perhaps, a number of questions were put in some states and not in others. Any idea why this was so?

DISCUSSION

1   I suppose the first thing that strikes one is that virtually all states in Europe chose a date in December as their census day. Ireland and the UK rather stick

out like sore thumbs in this regard. A Sunday round about the beginning of April had been the preferred option for those two countries since 1851. In 1841 the date had been 6 June. This had been abandoned principally because it was discovered that many people were away from their usual residence by June, either doing seasonal work (principally in agriculture) or on holiday. For instance, Margate's 'population' dropped between 1841 and 1851 because in the former year the town was already into its summer season (Whyman 1996, p.69). On the only other occasion when a summer census was held (20 June 1921) only 27,740 of Margate's total enumerated population of 46,480 were judged to be resident (Whyman, 1996, p. 56).

Table 1 Questions asked in the censuses of various European states ca.1870–80[1]

Questions \ State	Finland	Sweden	Norway	Denmark	Germany	England, Scotland and Wales	Ireland	Netherlands	Belgium	France	Spain	Italy	Switzerland	Austria	Hungary	Serbia
Date of census	31/12/65	31/12/70	31/12/75	7/2/80	1/12/80	2/4/71	2/4/71	1/12/69	31/12/66	12/76	31/12/77	31/12/71	1/12/70	31/12/80	31/12/80	12/74
1 Surname and first name	✓	✓	✓	✓	✓	✓	✓	✓	✓	✓	✓	✓	✓	✓	✓	✓
2 Sex	✓	✓	✓	✓	✓	✓	✓	✓	✓	✓	✓	✓	✓	✓	✓	✓
3 Age[2]	✓	Y	Y	✓	D	✓	✓	D	D	Y	✓	✓	D	Y	D	✓
4 Relationship to head of family or household	—	✓	✓	✓	✓	✓	✓	✓	✓	✓	✓	✓	✓	✓	✓	✓
5 Civil status	✓	✓	✓	✓	✓	✓	✓	✓	✓	✓	✓	✓	✓	✓	✓	✓
6 Occupation	✓	✓	✓	✓	✓	✓	✓	✓	✓	✓	✓	✓	✓	✓	✓	✓
7 Religion	✓	✓	✓	✓	✓	—	✓	✓	—	—	✓	✓	✓	✓	✓	✓
8 Ethnicity (language spoken)	✓	✓	✓	—	—	—	✓	—	✓	—	✓	—	✓	✓	✓[3]	—
9 Ability to read and write	—	—	—	—	—	—	✓	—	✓	—	—	✓	—	✓	✓	✓
10 Legal domicile	—	✓	—	—	✓	—	—	—	—	✓	✓	—	✓	✓[4]	✓	—
11 Place of birth	—	✓	✓	✓	✓	✓	✓	✓	✓	✓	—	✓	—	✓	✓	✓

12 Duration of stay	—	—	✓	—	—	✓	✓	✓	✓	—
13 Duration of absence	—	—	✓	—	✓	✓	✓	✓	✓	—
14 Usual place of abode	—	—	—	—	✓	—	✓	✓	—	—
15 Blind	✓	✓	—	✓	—	✓	✓	✓	✓	—
16 Deaf and dumb	✓	✓	—	✓	—	✓	✓	✓	✓	—
17 Imbecile, idiot	✓	✓	—	✓	—	✓	✓	—	✓	—
18 Insane	✓	✓	—	✓	—	✓	✓	✓	✓	—

[1] Delegates to the International Statistical Congress in St Petersburg in 1872 considered that these questions were 'essential'. They also put forward other questions that did not carry this label.

[2] D = date of birth: Y = year of birth. Otherwise age given in years. Confusion sometimes caused over whether this was at last or next birthday.

[3] Mother tongue besides knowledge of that of the country.

[4] Whether one belonged to the 'parish' or not. For foreigners the country of origin to appear in the comments column.

Source: Based on Kőrösi, Joseph (1881) *Projet d'un Recensement du Monde. Etude de Statistique*, Paris, pp.42–3.

That other countries chose a date in December was also because, at that time, more people were likely to be 'at home', whether that term was legally determined or not, than at any other time. Knowing the size of the normally resident population of a place was increasingly important throughout Europe either because the census was used to produce vital statistics (birth, death and marriage rates) in different parts of the country (this was one of the main purposes of the UK census) or as a means of allocating or collecting state revenues (Thorvaldsen, 2005).

2   Of the 18 questions specified in Table 1, only five were asked in all the European countries listed; surname and first name; age (although note how this question was to be answered varied from country to country); civil status (i.e. whether one was single, married, widowed or divorced); and occupation. All but Finland asked for the relationship of an individual to the head of the household in which he or she resided (i.e. wife, son, daughter, servant, apprentice etc.).

These core questions reflect the central interests of the states that carried out the censuses every 10 years in the case of the UK and Ireland, but at shorter intervals in some other states. If we set aside the first question – surname and first name – which might be considered the organising device of nominatively based censuses, we see that sex, age, relationship to head of household, civil status and occupation can all be of use to the state, especially the nineteenth-century state with its growing concern for the welfare of its citizens. The unadorned head count, how many lived in a particular place (e.g. town, county, state) at a particular time, remained, however, the headline statistic. Indeed it was one of the reasons why the UK held its first census in 1801. As you will recall from Unit 17, the country was then at war, and naturally the government wanted to know what manpower it had to draw upon. The same was true in 1811, as this jubilant comment from *The Times* makes clear:

> These returns of increased population [the population of England and Wales had grown from 8, 893,000 in 1801 to 10,164,000 in 1811] must afford high satisfaction to every patriotic mind as shewing that the radical resources of the country have not been affected by the war which has lasted so long.
>
> *The Times*, 24 July 1811, 3e.

The need to know the size of the male population of a country for military purposes remained a concern of European states throughout the nineteenth century, although after Napoleon's defeat there was to be no comparable continent-wide mobilisation until the First World War. Of the major continental powers, France became increasingly worried that its population was failing to match the growth rate of Prussia and, in the latter years of the century, Germany.

It was, however, the increasing interest in the economic and social progress of a state that became the focus of attention of census takers. The censuses showed that throughout Europe populations were growing. Industrialisation was beginning and its concomitant, urbanisation. Even the early censuses with their simple head counts revealed where people were, what areas were growing and what were not, and as they all sought some indication of what occupations were being followed, what was happening to the economy, both locally and nationally.

The movement of the state into welfare programmes – remember the brief discussion of the new regulatory state in Unit 18 – was also a major incentive to produce more detailed and more accurate census taking. The first of these programmes resulted from Jenner's discovery of a safe method of vaccinating against smallpox. So grave was the disease and so widespread, with often fatal results, that his discovery was rapidly taken up, both by private individuals and public bodies. The first state to make vaccination compulsory for all its citizens was Bavaria in 1807. Denmark followed in 1810, Norway (then part of the Danish state) in 1811, Russia in 1812, Sweden in 1816 (Glynn and Glynn, 2004, p.134). Making something compulsory by law did not, however, mean that it was universally adopted overnight. Thus in Norway, we find that in the opening decade of the nineteenth century, 156 vaccinations per 1,000 births were carried out. By 1831–40, the figure was 581 and by 1815–60 it was 815 (Drake 1969, p.53). Not all countries made vaccination compulsory as quickly as the countries listed above. In England, for instance, progress was painfully slow. Even when vaccination was finally made compulsory in 1853, it took until 1871 before an effective system of implementation was agreed. Just how effective is revealed by the fact that in the 1870s around 95 per cent of eligible babies (some died before they could be vaccinated at the recommended time of three months) were successfully vaccinated (Drake, 2005).

Although governments had the last say in what questions were to be included in a census, the decision was subject to lobbying by particular interest groups. One of these was made up of the heads of Europe's state statistical office. These men first met in Brussels in 1853 and at the Statistical Congress held in St Petersburg in 1872 agreed a standard format for decadal censuses, presented above in Table 1. As we have seen not all the recommendations were accepted by all governments. Sometimes agreement could not be reached on how the question should be framed. Take religion, for example, almost all states had a question on this, but not the UK. This had not always been the case, for in 1851 a census of church/chapel attendance was taken. Although flawed in its execution, the result had been very pleasing for the nonconformists, for it revealed that attendance at their services was almost as high as at those of the Church of England. Thereafter, Anglicans lobbied for a census of religious persuasion, but this was successfully resisted. The issue had strong financial implications since annual grants for education were based on the number of Dissenters and Anglicans in the population (Drake 1972, pp.15–19).

Questions 10–14 are all related to the important issue of internal migration. Successive censuses revealed the extent of this, especially from rural to urban areas. Again, as with religious affiliation, where a person belonged could have financial implications, in terms of tax receipts and government grants. Residence also had implications for electoral purposes.

Finally, questions 15–18 were included in a surprising number of censuses, surprising because relatively few people were involved, getting meaningful replies was difficult if not impossible, and, in the case of the UK at least, no useful purpose seems to have been served.

HOW CENSUSES WERE TAKEN

Conducting a census was a major undertaking, involving a considerable number of people not only to administer it, but also to make the tabulations. Some states used existing bodies to carry out both these aspects of the work. For example, in England and Wales, the censuses of 1801, 1811, 1821 and 1831, all of which were head counts, were carried out by the overseers of the poor. This was cheap but unsatisfactory as the standardisation of procedures was virtually impossible (Drake, 1972, p.24). From 1841 onwards, following a separate act of parliament for each census, a special organisation was set up which employed many thousands of enumerators who distributed, collected and then copied the census forms into what are now known as the Census Enumerators' Books (CEBs). This work was carried out under the supervision of the 2,000 or more Superintendent Registrars of Births, Deaths and Marriages, an office created in 1837. Both the forms and the CEBs were sent to London where an army of temporary clerks carried out the tabulations. This huge task was done manually. The US Census of 1890 was the first to use a mechanical device, the Hollerith machine for sorting punched cards, a precursor of today's computer. But although Hollerith himself offered to pay the travelling expenses of someone associated with the UK census, someone who would come to the USA and examine his machine, there is no evidence that the invitation was taken up (Drake, 1972, p.15).

The sheer amount of work involved in processing the CEBs meant that only a limited amount of analysis could be carried out. Today, anyone with a computer and the ability to use a spreadsheet program can produce far more information – as we shall see – than could the census takers of the nineteenth century. In fact, given the limitations of what could be done with the available technology, it is rather surprising that so many questions appeared on the census form.

ASHFORD AND TROMSØ

We shall now bring our discussion of the census down from the general to the particular, by examining the CEBs from two small towns: Ashford in Kent and Tromsø, some 250 miles inside the Arctic Circle in the north of Norway. We are doing this for several reasons. First, as indicated in Table 1, we seek to demonstrate that the governments of England and Norway were interested in certain basic information as shown by Tables 2 and 3.

Table 2 Rubric of the census form for Ashford 1851

LIST of the MEMBERS of this FAMILY, of VISITORS, and of SERVANTS who SLEPT or ABODE in this HOUSE on the NIGHT of SUNDAY, MARCH 30th

NAME and SURNAME	RELATION	CONDITION	SEX	AGE	RANK, PROFESSION or OCCUPATION	WHERE BORN	If Deaf-and-Dumb or Blind
No person absent on the Night of March 30th to be entered Write after the Name of the Head of the Family, the Names of his Wife, Children, and others of the same Surname; then Visitors, Servants etc.	To head of Family. State whether Wife, Son, Daughter, or other Relative, Visitor or Servant	Write 'Married', 'Widower', 'Widow', or 'Unmarried' against the Names of all Persons except young children	Write 'M' against Males and 'F' against Females	(Last birthday) For infants under One Year, state the Age in Months, writing 'Under 1 month', '1 month', '2 months' etc	*(Before filling in this Column you are requested to read the Instructions on the other side)*	Opposite the Names of those born in England, write the *County*, and *Town* or *Parish* If born in Scotland, Ireland, the British Colonies, the East Indies, or in Foreign Parts, state the Country; in the last case, if a British Subject, add, *'British Subject'*	Write 'Deaf-and-Dumb' or 'Blind', opposite the name of the Person.

Table 3 Rubric of the census form for Tromsø 1865

Household	First name and surname	Relationship in family; head, wife, son, daughter, parents, servants, lodgers together with each one's status or occupation	Unmarried, married, widower, widow or divorced	Age last birthday	Birthplace i.e. town or village and in the latter case the parish or county name. If born abroad state the country	Religious affiliation if other than the State Church	Insane, deaf and dumb or blind. If insane state whether from birth or not. If blind state whether can see to walk	Total population in each house
				Male				
				Female				

Livestock numbers at 31st December 1865

Horses	Cattle	Sheep	Goats	Pigs	Hens

Quantity of seed (toenne = 4 bushels)

Wheat	Rye	Barley	Mixed grains	Oats	Peas	Potatoes

This as not all the information sought. For instance, in 1851, the English wanted to know if a person was deaf and dumb, an imbecile or insane, whilst the Norwegian enquired as to the number and type of livestock in a household.

EXERCISE

A second reason for inviting you to examine the census returns of two different communities is neatly expressed in this quotation from Rudyard Kipling's poem 'The English Flag', 'And what should they know of England who only England know?'. My argument is, then, that by examining two or more places, institutions or histories together one can get a better grasp of their essence. Look, for example, at Tables 4 and 5. Concentrate first on the names of the streets. What are the similarities and the differences?

Table 4   Number of resident domestic servants in Tromsø by street, 1865

Street	Servants
Back Street	7
Customs House Street	10
Green Street	23
Hill Street	
Latin School House	1
Main Street	82
North Church Street	17
North Shore Street	48
North Shore Street (Bay)	1
Prison on the Market Place	2
River Street	
Sea Street	25
South Church Street	3
South Shore Street	36
The Hill	
The Shore	2
West Street	22
Wharf Street	2
	281

Table 5   Number of resident domestic servants in Ashford by street, 1851

Street	Servants
Alfred New Town	16
Back lane	
Barrow Hill	10
Barrow hill (Top)	
Barrow Hill Cottages	2
Barrow Hill Place	5
Barrow Hill Place (Back)	
Barrow hill Row	
Barrow hill Terrace	9
Barrow hill Villa	
Beaver	1
Beaver Green	5
Bridge Street	15
Brook Place	3
Castle Street	8
Chart Road	
Church Yard	4
Cottage in Field	
Dover Road	5
Dover Place	6
Drum Lane	3
Drum Lane (East)	3
Faversham Road	2
Forge Lane	
Gravel Pit Street	4
Gravel Walk	2
Hempstead Place	2
High Street	29
High Street (East Hill)	3
High Street (North Side)	35
High Street (South Side)	60
Kingsnorth Road	
Knatchbull Place	
Maarsh Street	6
Middle Row	9

New Rents	14
New Street	27
North Street	20
Prospect place	
Railway Station	2
Sandhurst Lane	6
St. John's Lane	1
Station Road	5
Stevens Cottages	
Warren Lane	
Whist Lane	2
	324

DISCUSSION

What struck me immediately was that Tromsø had far fewer streets, or perhaps, we should say, addresses, since in both cases there are one or two individual buildings named, than did Ashford. Admittedly the same street appeared under different heads in Ashford, for example, High Street. But even allowing for this there were more streets in Ashford than in Tromsø. In part this was because Ashford in 1851 was somewhat larger than Tromsø in 1865, with its enumerated population of 4,983 as against 4,073. Also Ashford was a much older town than Tromsø. The latter had been formally created by the state in 1794, whilst the former had its origins in the Middle Ages. Not only was the state involved in the creation and/or designation of a town in Norway, it also was involved in its layout. Thus whereas in Ashford, as in most English towns, the layout of streets was determined by local interests – landowners, landlords, developers – over time, Tromsø's streets were for the most part set out in a grid pattern well in advance of their being built upon. You might also have noted that the street names of Tromsø were less varied than those of Ashford and frequently reflected their geographical location, for example, The Shore North and South Shore Street, West Street, North and South Wharf Street. The two towns did, however, have a number of street names in common – Church Street, High Street/Main Street, Back street/Back lane.

Turn now to the other feature of Tables 4 and 5: the location of domestic servants in the two towns. Again what strikes you?

What is immediately apparent is that the residences of the domestic servants were not distributed randomly. They were concentrated in certain streets. In Ashford the High Street stands out, with over two out of five of the town's servants living there (127/324). There were more servants too living in its counterpart in Tromsø (Main Street) than anywhere else, although the proportion was less, about three out of ten, or 82 out of 281. These numbers and proportions reflect the development of the two towns. Both were pre-industrial in the sense that their better-off inhabitants (the ones who could afford domestic servants) lived on their main streets that were in their town centres. Today, of course, the better-off tend to live on the outskirts of towns. That Tromsø had a relatively large number of servants living on streets that bordered the sea – South Shore Street and Sea Street – was because some of the town's richest merchants lived there, across the road from their warehouses. Again this is a pre-industrial or early industrial characteristic.

You should now turn to the *Media Book* and continue this work with Tutorial 4 on the CD-ROM.

REFERENCES

Drake, M. (1969) *Population and Society in Norway, 1735–1865,* Cambridge, Cambridge University Press.

Drake, M. (1972) 'The census 1801–1891' in E.A. Wrigley, *Nineteenth-Century Society: Essays in the use of Quantitative Methods for the Study of Social Data*, Cambridge, Cambridge University Press.

Drake, M. (2005) 'The Vaccination Registers: what they are and what we can learn from them', *Local Population Studies*, 74, pp.36–53.

Glynn, I. and J. (2004) *The life and death of smallpox*, London, Profile.

Mills, D. and Schürer, K. (eds) *Local Communities in the Victorian Census Enumerators'* Books, Oxford, Leopard's Head Press.

Thorvaldsen, G. (2005) 'Away on census day. Enumerating the temporarily present or absent', Unpublished manuscript.

The Times, 24 July 1811.

Whyman, J. (1996) 'Visitors to Margate in the 1841 census: an attempt to look at the age and social structure of Victorian holidaymaking', in Mills, D and Schürer, K.

FURTHER READING

Unit 17

Sperber, J. (2000) *Revolutionary Europe, 1780–1850*, London, Longman.

Unit 18

Sperber, J. (2000) *Revolutionary Europe, 1780–1850*, London, Longman.

Unit 19

Armstrong, J. (1982) *Nations before Nationalism*, Chapel Hill, University of North Carolina Press.

Baycroft, T. (1995) 'Peasants into Frenchmen? The case of the Flemish in the north of France 1860–1914', *European Review of History*, vol. 2, no. 1, pp.31–44.

Ford, C. (1993) *Creating the Nation in Provincial France*, Princeton, Princeton University Press.

Unit 20

Black, J. and MacRaild, D. (2000) *Studying History*, London, Macmillan.

Hobsbawm, E. and Ranger, T. (eds) (1983) *The Invention of Tradition,* Cambridge, Cambridge University Press.

Hutchinson, J. (1994) *Modern Nationalism*, London, Fontana.

Kedourie, E. (1983) *Nationalism*, Oxford, Blackwell.

Lawrence, P. (2004) *Nationalism. History and Theory*, Harlow, Pearson.

Nimni, E. (1985) 'Great historical failure: Marxist theories of nationalism', *Capital and Class*, vol. 25, pp. 58–83.

Parker, C. (1990) *The English Historical Tradition since 1850*, Edinburgh, John Donald.

Raphael, L. (2000) 'Flexible response? Strategies of academic historians towards larger markets for national historiographies and increasing scientific standards' in *An Assessment of Twentieth Century Historiography*, KVHAA *Konferenser 49*, Stockholm.

Smith, A.D. (1992) 'Nationalism and the historians', *International Journal of Comparative Sociology*, vol. 33, no. 1–2, pp. 58–80.

Stuchtey, B. and Wende, P. (eds) (2000) *British and German Historiography, 1750–1950 – Traditions, Perceptions, and Transfers*, Oxford, Oxford University Press.

Weber, M. (1948) 'The nation' in Gerth, H. and Wright Mills, C. (eds) *From Max Weber. Essays in Sociology*, London, Kegan Paul.

Xenos, N. (1993) 'Nations, state and economy: Max Weber's Freiburg inaugural lecture' in Ringrose, M. and Lerner, A.J. (eds) *Reimagining the Nation*, Buckingham, Open University Press.

GLOSSARY

Acte additionnel **(French)**
Additions, broadly liberal in tone, made to the imperial constitution during the **Hundred Days**.

auditeur **(French)**
A young official of Napoleon's Council of State. Usually the first rung on the ladder to senior appointments in the imperial administration.

Befreiungskrieg **(German)**
The German war of liberation from Napoleon, 1813–14.

bourgeoisie
In Marxist theory, the bourgeoisie are that class of people who live off the capital they possess. By renting property or owning factories they thus make a living without working themselves.

Bund (Deutsche Bund) **(German)**
The federation of independent German states established following the Congress of Vienna.

carabinieri reali **(Italian)**
Literally 'royal rifles'; the Italian variant of the *gendarmerie*.

Chartism
British working-class movement, taking its name from the People's Charter (published in May 1838) that demanded: male suffrage; equal electoral districts; voting by ballot; abolition of property qualifications for MPs; payment for MPs; annual parliaments. Petitions were presented to parliament for the Charter in 1839, 1842 and 1848.

Combination Acts
Legislation to consolidate other acts and to speed up the prosecution of people acting in restraint of trade – this technically included masters, but principally was directed against workers 'combinations' (or embryonic trade unions). The first act was passed in 1799 and amended in 1800. The acts were repealed in 1824 but, following a wave of strikes, new restrictive measures were introduced in 1825. Similar legislation was introduced in France in 1791 with the Le Chapelier Law.

commissaire (de police) **(French)**
Often translated as 'commissioner'. The principal police officer of a French town; larger towns had several (in Paris from the Revolution to the restoration of the monarchy there were forty-eight).

Corn Laws
Legislation placing duties on corn introduced to protect the landed interest following the collapse of artificially high prices caused by the Napoleonic wars. The key legislation was passed in 1815. It was repealed in 1846 following agitation by the Anti-Corn Law League (middle-class supporters of free trade, with working-class support) and the Irish potato famine.

département (French)

The principal administrative unit of France (and the Napoleonic empire) established during the Revolution. In 1800, there were 98 départements; at its peak, the Napoleonic empire had 130.

émigré (French)

An individual who sought refuge outside France during the Revolution, not necessarily a noble.

gendarmerie (French)

Military police generally deployed for the maintenance of order in the French countryside. The *gendarmerie* was reorganised out of an older police system during the Revolution and exported across Europe behind the French armies.

Great Reform Act

The first Parliamentary Reform Act passed in 1832 against a background of political unrest and disorder. The Act increased the electorate from about 435,000 to 652,000 and gave political importance to the fast-growing industrial towns of the Midlands and the north. It gave uniformity to the franchise (40 shilling freeholders in the counties and borough householders paying an annual rent of £10). But in so doing it disfranchised some working-class voters in those old constituencies with a wide franchise. The working class as a whole was excluded by the legislation, leading to bitterness among activists and contributing to the rise of Chartism.

historiography

The writing of history, or the history of history writing

Hundred Days

The period of Napoleon's return from exile on Elba in 1815, during which the empire was briefly restored. The Hundred Days ended with Napoleon's defeat at Waterloo (18 June) and second abdication (22 June).

Jacobins

A radical faction during the French Revolution, generally associated with the 'Terror' regime of 1793–94.

Junkers (German)

Nobles and gentry of Prussia.

la grande nation (French)

Literally 'the great nation'; a term popular in France for describing France towards the end of the 1790s.

levée en masse (French)

The attempt by the French revolutionary government to organise the entire population for war in 1793.

proletariat

In Marxist theory, the proletariat are the working class – those whose sole means of income is the sale of their labour.

restoration (France/Europe)

The term used to describe France (or Europe) in the generation after Napoleon's downfall and the restoration of, principally, the Bourbon monarchy in France.

***Risorgimento* (Italian)**

Literally meaning 'resurrection', and named after the journal *Il Risorgimento*, this was the term used to describe the process of Italian unification.

romanticism

A broad cultural and intellectual movement that swept Europe in the period 1775–1830. Romantic themes included a desire to 'return to nature', a belief in the essential goodness of humanity and the development of national pride in place of cosmopolitanism.

Vendée

The *département* in western France that became the centre of royalist insurrection against the Revolution prompted by restrictions on the church and military levies for the war.

'Whig' interpretation of history

An uncritical mode of history writing, which takes the present as a desirable and inevitable norm and merely traces the rise of present conditions, conveniently ignoring other elements of the past.

***Zelanti* (Italian)**

Ardent supporters of conservative politics in the Papal States during the early years of the restoration.

***Zollverein* (German)**

A customs union of German states.

INDEX